MARITIME STRIKE

The Untold Story of the Royal Navy Task
Group off Libya in 2011

REAR ADMIRAL JOHN KINGWELL CBE

CASEMATE

Oxford & Philadelphia

Published in the Great Britain and the United States of America in 2022 by
CASEMATE PUBLISHERS
The Old Music Hall, 106–108 Cowley Road, Oxford OX4 1JE, UK
and
1950 Lawrence Road, Havertown, PA 19083, USA

Copyright 2022 © John Kingwell.
Maps created by Alix Kingwell.

Hardback Edition: ISBN 978-1-63624-113-5
Digital Edition: ISBN 978-1-63624-114-2

A CIP record for this book is available from the British Library

Printed and bound in the United Kingdom by TJ Books

Typeset in India by Lapiz Digital Services, Chennai.

For a complete list of Casemate titles, please contact:

CASEMATE PUBLISHERS (UK)
Telephone (01865) 241249
Email: casemate-uk@casematepublishers.co.uk
www.casematepublishers.co.uk

CASEMATE PUBLISHERS (US)
Telephone (610) 853-9131
Fax (610) 853-9146
Email: casemate@casematepublishers.com
www.casematepublishers.com

Cover image: 12th May 2011, a Replinshment at Sea (RAS) took place for HMS Ocean (right)
and HMS Albion (left) with RFA Fort Rosalie (centre), in preparation for Cougar 11 exercise
Cypriot Lion. Available under Open Government Licence version 1.0 at: https://commons.
wikimedia.org/wiki/File:HMS_Albion,_RFA_Fort_Rosalie_and_HMS_Ocean_Conduct_a_
Replenishment_at_Sea_During_Ex_Cypriot_Lion_MOD_45152750.jpg

Contents

Foreword

The main focus of effort in the Ministry of Defence in early 2011 was success in Afghanistan and dealing with the outcome of a truly horrendous Defence Spending Review. The Arab Spring and its consequences came as a shock to the system and the international politics of the day swiftly required our force planners to make contingency plans to satisfy the need to 'do something'. As the then First Sea Lord and Chief of Naval Staff, I was only too aware of the pressure on all our forces but particularly the Royal Navy where contingency tasking from Afghanistan through the Middle East and Mediterranean to the Caribbean was significantly stretching the Fleet and its manpower. The recently formed Response Force Task Group (RFTG) concept was in the earliest stages of preparedness but was the designated deployable headquarters to command whatever forces the planning required. With Commodore John Kingwell as its designated Commander UK Task Group (COMUKTG) the RFTG was going to be tested much earlier than was previously envisioned.

This book, authored by John, gives a detailed account of how well this rapid generation of the RFTG was achieved and a comprehensive insight, warts and all, into the execution of the subsequent mission it conducted, Operation *Ellamy*, which was the name given to the UK's response to the uprising and civil war in Libya against the Gaddafi regime.

John's personal journey, from dustman's son to senior naval commander, which is covered in some detail, gives an important insight into his career path, each phase of which contributed to the experience that underpinned the leadership required of him as the commander of forces on live operations. The detailed documenting of his thinking, not just at the operational level but taking into account the thought processes of his 'one and two up commanders', gives a high-level insight into the workings of a truly integrated command structure. Another success criterion he covers is the web of personality-based relationships that are so fundamental to the smooth running of an operation. This was especially important for the *Ellamy* RFTG as a consequence of the plethora of linked command and control structures that oversaw the wider international and NATO response to the Libyan civil war. Kingwell is very open and frank in his analysis of each of these relationships and the successes that they brought as well as the friction and inertia that were generated by some.

What stands out for me in this very readable account is the success of the RFTG as a vehicle of defence demonstrating that it was able, at very short notice and with a comprehensively trained and correctly constituted battle staff, to deliver a suite of options to be utilised as the changing circumstances dictated. Such capability is only achievable through a ceaseless training regime, the right equipment and people all overseen by experienced leadership.

John Kingwell was lucky and was in the right place at an opportune time. His career journey was far from unique, but it fell to him as the COMUKTG at the time to utilise all the training and experience of his previous service. He emerged, having at one point been threatened with the sack, as a proven commander of significant standing and in possession of the greatest operational experience of his generation.

The book is a rich source of information, lessons learnt and examples of how to deliver operational success as well as of the pitfalls of maritime and joint command at the operational level. It is an engaging and informative read for all those aspiring to command at the same level or simply interested in the story of Operation *Ellamy* and the career journey of one of the Royal Navy's most talented officers.

Admiral Sir Mark Stanhope GCB, OBE
Chief of Naval Staff and First Sea Lord 2009–2013

Preface

In the spring and summer of 2011, a force of 10 ships, a nuclear submarine, a Lead Commando Group and Royal Navy and Army helicopters were deployed into the Mediterranean in response to the instability caused by the Arab Spring uprisings. *Maritime Strike* tells the story of the Response Force Task Group (RFTG), which for 170 days provided options to respond to the developing situation in Libya, Syria and Yemen, and played an important part in the campaign that resulted in the downfall of Gaddafi.

From June it planned 47, and launched 22, Apache missions against Gaddafi's forces in order to protect the Libyan civilian population. This was defence at its best, offering choice to government against a range of contingencies and later, off Libya, launching Army helicopters from Royal Navy ships, supported by Navy helicopters as part of a wider air campaign. It included a number of significant firsts – of Apache helicopters striking from the sea and the first operational embarkation of US Air Force HH-60 helicopters and combat search and rescue teams in a Royal Navy ship.

The men and women of the Task Group achieved remarkable things, and part of my reason for writing this book was to ensure that their contribution was captured and retold, since at the time inter-service agendas and misunderstandings resulted in much of the Task Group's contribution being largely unreported. In addition, command and commanding a Task Group on operations is a deeply personal activity and this book also tells my story as Commander of the UK Task Group. I wanted to explain how the Royal Navy enabled and prepared a dustman's son from the Elephant and Castle to command its Task Group at sea and also recount what it was actually like to be COMUKTG in those challenging months.

In doing this I am extremely fortunate to have kept detailed journals of my time in command, be it of ships or of the Task Group itself, on which I was able to draw extensively. In addition, I have also drawn on contemporary newspaper reports, and some accounts of the RFTG published after 2011. For those interested in the higher strategic/operational aspects of the period I recommend Brigadier Rob Weighill and Florence Gaub's book, *The Cauldron*, which covers the NATO campaign. If your interest is the tactical aspects of Apache operations, I heartily recommend Will Laidlaw's *Apache over Libya*, and I was grateful to be able to refer to both books.

This book should not be regarded as a comprehensive account of the Libya campaign nor indeed of the Royal Navy's contribution to it – rather it is a very personal account of my experience commanding at sea in a complex joint and international setting. As my journal entry for 3 June recounts: 'Probably the most demanding evening of my service. For the first time in 27 years, I order ships and aircraft into action with the very real possibility of killing the enemy and losing people.'

In writing this I hope to have captured the majority of the Royal Navy effort and have provided an insight into the professionalism and dedication of all those – from all three services – that played such an important part in delivering maritime strike. At the core of this capability were the men and women of the integrated COMUKTG/3 Commando Brigade and Army Air Corps battle staff – both in HMS *OCEAN* and HMS *ALBION* – who meticulously planned our missions and potential operations, together with the various ships, submarines and squadrons that contributed to the campaign. I particularly want to highlight the bravery of each of the Apache pilots who dealt with the dangers of operating at low level over the sea at night as well as facing (and being engaged by) the most advanced shoulder-launched anti-aircraft missiles and gunfire. Finally, any omissions are entirely unintentional and in no way detract from the magnificent contribution that every ship, squadron, submarine, the Lead Commando Group and individual made.

Bexhill-on-Sea, 2022

CHAPTER ONE

Preparation for Command

The Royal Navy (RN) was a way of life for me for some 36 years during which I served as a warfare officer. Looking back I now realise that one of the great strengths of the Navy is the way in which it prepares its officers for command and specifically warfare officers for command at sea. Indeed, every step of a career is preparing you for what may come next. And yet despite this, the 16-year-old who rather nervously entered the careers office in Croydon, South London, had no real ambition, nor expectation, to one day command at sea. My family had no connections with the sea, or indeed military service. My father was a dustman and my mother a waitress and we lived in rented flats, initially in Brixton and then the New Kent Road in the Elephant and Castle. My interest in joining the Navy had been sparked by joining the Sea Cadets, having seen some cadets in naval uniform. It seemed to me that the Navy might offer some prospect of a career and, if I am being honest, an escape from run-down central London of the 1980s. By the time I was 15 I was determined to join the Navy not as an officer, which to me seemed to me unattainable for a working-class kid like me, but as a gunnery rating.

And so I set off for the Croydon careers office, where a chief petty officer told me that since I was taking O levels early I would be overqualified to be a gunner – and that was that, I should consider an alternative career. Undeterred, I simply got on a bus to the next nearest recruiting office which was at High Holborn. Here, another chief gave me the same message but asked me to wait and see a WRNS officer who was responsible for recruiting officers. She told me that although it was highly unlikely that I would be accepted as an officer – since I had the wrong family background – I should nonetheless work hard at school, achieve A levels and apply to get a University Cadetship. This form of entry was highly sought after since it meant joining the Navy and, after a year, going to university on full pay. I would have to gain a place at university (which would be a first for anyone in my family) and appear at the Admiralty Interview Board (AIB) for two days of tests and interviews. And although she could not see me being offered a cadetship I might have an outside chance of a short career commission.

Eighteen months later a 17-year-old Kingwell appeared at the AIB at HMS *SULTAN* in Portsmouth with an offer to study history at Loughborough in the bag. For me the most unsettling aspect of the experience was being told by one of the other, rather posh, candidates that my shirts (white collar and coloured body) were completely inappropriate – and I feared that the board would somehow assume that my father had got them from his dust round – which he had! Despite this apparent fashion faux pas, unlike the candidate who had offered the advice, I passed the AIB and – to my great surprise – was indeed offered a University Cadetship beginning with the September 1984 entry at Dartmouth.

As a University Cadet I was effectively only at Dartmouth for just over three months – followed by a further three months spent at sea in the Dartmouth training ship – before returning in April to pass out. Although the Sea Cadets had in many ways prepared me for joining the Navy as a rating I found Dartmouth challenging in that I had little in common with many of the other officer cadets who were older (I was just 18) and had very different backgrounds. Dartmouth in 1984 had the feel of a large public school, with which many of my fellow cadets were familiar but which to me was very alien. I was even sent to elocution lessons to temper my London accent. I simply focused on being in the right place at the right time and passing the very regular tests that came my way and marked the end of each phase of training. Unsurprisingly imposter syndrome was alive and well; I found it hard to believe that I was actually at Dartmouth and at times wondered if I really should have been a gunner.

That said, the Dartmouth experience achieves its aims of creating potential officers and leaders in very subtle but effective ways. No one who passes out of the College can fail to gain a sense of the Royal Navy's place in the nation's history and its role safeguarding the nation's security. During the countless hours spent on the parade ground we looked up at the inscription on the College that proudly proclaims that 'it is upon the Royal Navy that the nation's wealth, prosperity and peace depend'. And we were very aware that we were following in the footsteps of our illustrious predecessors since the college's main corridor was lined with passing out photographs of every entry since 1905. I also count myself very fortunate to have been in Cunningham division which was guided by Lieutenant Commander Paddy Watson, whose absolute standards left an enduring impression on me – and indeed all of my fellow officer cadets. So, the young man who stood for the final time on the parade ground at Dartmouth in April 1985 was both fitter and more confident than he had been just a few months earlier and was well prepared to join the Navy proper and his first ship.

I joined the Leander-class frigate HMS *APOLLO* in Devonport dockyard on 30 April 1985 for what was known as fleet training. The five of us[1] who joined from Dartmouth were known as Officers Under Training (OUT), spending our time completing task books that required us to work in, and get to know, every department in the ship. We also took turns understudying the officer of the day who was responsible for the safety of the ship in harbour and for the first time lived as members of the wardroom, as the officers' mess in ships is called. This required us for the first time to occasionally take charge of, and most importantly work with, ratings. If I had endured Dartmouth I loved being in a ship, and thrived there. The goal of training was a Fleetboard examination in which we would be tested on our knowledge of every aspect of the ship in a day of oral examinations, the successful passing of which would mean commissioning into the Navy. For my fellow OUTs this would be in September but for me the autumn would see me going to Loughborough with my Fleetboard taking place after university in 1989. So, I had the real benefit of time to learn and a lack of pressure.

In 1985 *APOLLO* was emerging from refit. As she was only 16 years old this should have been its mid-life update, originally planned to see the 1950s-designed armament and sensors replaced with more modern equivalents including Sea Wolf anti-air and Exocet anti-ship missiles. However, these conversions, at some £70M[2] per ship, were expensive, and the 1981 Defence review cancelled the refits of the last 5 ships on cost grounds. As a result, *APOLLO* returned to sea in its original – somewhat outdated – configuration. The ship's operation room had no automatic data handling system and relied on manual plotting of radar contacts. The ship was armed with a twin 4.5in gun, Sea Cat surface-to-air missile system, an anti-submarine mortar and a Wasp helicopter.

I had the benefit of witnessing and taking part in sea trials and operational sea training (OST) – all under the supportive guidance of *APOLLO*'s captain, Commander Jeremy De Halpert. I enjoyed my time in *APOLLO* to the extent that I was in many ways disappointed to have to leave the ship in August to go to university, but the Captain arranged for me to be affiliated to the ship for my summer training periods and as a result I spent each summer onboard until graduating, when I was to return permanently with the aim of completing my sea training.

My final four months in *APOLLO* were therefore in the summer of 1988. By then I knew the ship very well and I had already been to sea in the previous year with Jeremy's replacement, Commander Laurie Hopkins. *APOLLO* was reaching the end of its service with the RN and was to be transferred to Pakistan in October, which meant that the ship was losing many of its officers prior to transfer. Laurie Hopkins showed huge confidence in me by effectively ending my training and employing me as a qualified officer. I was no longer an understudy but had my own watch at sea and my own division of sailors to look after as the acting Signal Communication Officer. *APOLLO* transferred to the Pakistan Navy at a moving handover ceremony at Portsmouth Naval Base on 14 October 1988 and I departed complete with certificates of confidence as an Officer of the Day and as an Officer of the Watch (Daylight) – the only snag being that I had yet to take the Fleetboard examination that is the normal prerequisite for what I had been doing in *APOLLO* for last four months.

The day after the handover I flew to Dubai to join *APOLLO*'s sister ship HMS *JUPITER* for three months' intensive revision prior to the dreaded board. *JUPITER* was three years older than *APOLLO* and had undergone the full mid-life modernisation update intended for the class. As a result, although she had the same propulsion system as her younger sister she had an automated operations room and was equipped with Sea Wolf and Exocet missiles, anti-submarine torpedo tubes and a Lynx helicopter. So there was much to learn. Not only this, but I had the opportunity to experience deployed operations at sea for the first time since *JUPITER* was deployed to the Gulf on the *Armilla* patrol at the tail end of the Iran–Iraq war. The ship handed over its *Armilla* duties with the traditional steam past of the incoming Task Group (HM Ships *BRAZEN, BOXER* and *BIRMINGHAM*) on 11 November and began its passage to Portsmouth. *JUPITER*'s captain was Commander Jock Moodie and once again a supportive captain enabled me to prepare thoroughly for, and arranged for me to attend, the first available Fleetboard on the ship's return to the UK. An added bonus was the chance to complete my Ocean Navigation Certificate during the ship's passage from the Persian Gulf to the Red Sea, establishing that I could navigate without modern navigational aids but by sextant.

I sat the Fleetboard on 2 February 1989 and passed with flying colours – and was now a commissioned naval officer. The change in me since joining Dartmouth was huge and I certainly felt that I was now capable of being a good junior naval officer – the imposter syndrome was at least in this regard gone. I had been fortunate in these early years to serve in two great ships with three really supportive captains. While most of my contemporaries had nine months of training before their boards I had enjoyed 16 months (thanks to returning to sea during the summers) and in *APOLLO* had been trusted with my own day watch and division. When my success at Fleetboard was announced I received a note from Laurie Hopkins – it was succinct as always and described me as a 'smart arse'!

Next step in the path to what is known as a complement appointment – when you are on the trained strength – was four months of professional courses based at HMS *DRYAD* near Portsmouth. While Fleet training had had a whole-ship focus, covering every department onboard, the Officer of the Watch courses were specifically designed to prepare officers for their first complement job – which for a warfare officer revolves around safely navigating and manoeuvring a ship at sea, on behalf of and under the supervision of the captain. Largely land-based, the course's highlight was the Navigation Sea Week – at that time in the converted trawler *NORTHELLA* – in which your ability to conduct coastal navigation was put to the test.

At the end of the course we were appointed to our first jobs in the Navy and I was to join the Rosyth-based Type 42 Destroyer HMS *EDINBURGH*, relieving none other than HRH the Duke of York. *EDINBURGH* was the youngest and last of the class and was only four years old when I joined. Designed to provide area air defence for the Fleet, she was armed with the Sea Dart missile system, a 4.5in gun, anti-submarine torpedo tubes and a Lynx helicopter. I joined the ship on 27 June and was met by a friendly and welcoming Prince Andrew who in the next two weeks helped me settle into the ship and handed over his various responsibilities. In addition to taking over H's (as he was known) division of sailors I was also to be the Correspondence Officer (known as CORRO) dealing with the ship's and captain's regular correspondence. As CORRO I had the great benefit of working more closely with the Captain than most of the junior officers onboard did and gained a real insight into naval administration. This was particularly the case since *EDINBURGH* had a four-ring captain (Captain Alistair Ross) with an eye for detail and a wealth of experience to learn from.

My main task was to gain my Bridge Watchkeeping Certificate which would enable me to stand my own watch at sea by both day and night. The challenge was that this usually took at least six months at sea, and often more, with the same captain – and Captain Ross was due to hand over command in November, only five months after my joining. On the plus side *EDINBURGH* was part of the NATO Standing Force

Atlantic, known as STANAVFORLANT, a group of seven destroyers and frigates[3] with the flagship being the German frigate *EMDEN*. As a result, we were in close company with a formation of ships, enabling me to quickly become comfortable with handling *EDINBURGH* as part of a Task Group and quickly and safely taking station on other ships when ordered. Real highlights of this apprenticeship were taking the ship through the strong tidal stream of the Skagerrak and Kattegat in formation at night – the second time being far more comfortable than the first – and being on watch through the narrowest part of the English Channel. In November 1989 I was awarded the treasured Bridge Watchkeeping Certificate.

STANAVFORLANT spent most of its time preparing to meet the Soviet threat and hopefully contributing to deterring possible Soviet aggression. This had been a major theme of my early naval experience – in *APOLLO* I had taken part in a number of NATO North Atlantic exercises against a simulated Soviet Northern Fleet and at *DRYAD* we had studied the Soviet capabilities that we might one day face. This all changed when the Berlin Wall fell on 9 November. Unlike 9/11, in 1989 there were no TV pictures or social media available at sea and the news came by signal. The strategic implications were powerfully brought home to us by the hugely impressive NATO Task Group Commander, German Rear Admiral K. D. Laudien, who visited each ship in turn to speak to the officers. His message was profound: his country, the world and our professions had changed for good – an early lesson about the value of Task Group commanders personally passing on key news.

EDINBURGH left STANAVFORLANT and returned to Rosyth at the end of the year with a new captain, Commander Andrew Dickson. The ship entered a short docking period that saw hull-stiffening beams fitted to the ship's sides and a single 20mm Phalanx point defence system fitted on the forecastle in between the 4.5in gun and Sea Dart launcher. *EDINBURGH* was to be the only Type 42 destroyer to be fitted with this arrangement, which was designed to free up the midship area for the eventual fitting of lightweight Sea Wolf systems.[4]

We returned to sea in the summer for sea trials and training before undergoing operational sea training at the end of 1990. This OST would be particularly challenging – we had a number of new faces, many without recent experience of being in frigate or destroyer, let alone a Type 42, and I was the only qualified watchkeeping officer alongside our navigator, Lieutenant Andy Horner. Long days followed, with me mainly on the bridge as Officer of the Watch and occasionally standing in for Andy, enabling him to get on with planning. Bridge time was interrupted by action stations when I ran the Forrard Section Base. Looking back, it was great experience both in terms of handling the ship and pilotage but also the direct leadership style required to direct damage control and firefighting teams.

As my time in *EDINBURGH* came to an end the plan (and certainly Captain Ross) saw me going to navigate a frigate next. However, my appointer called and said that he felt that with all the bridge experience that I had recently gained I would benefit more from being second in command of a smaller ship. He even rather apologetically asked if I would mind going to the Fishery Protection Squadron with all the clambering in and out of seaboats that that would involve. I, rather predictably, jumped at the chance and was duly appointed as the executive officer (XO or first lieutenant) of the Ton-class minehunter HMS *SHERATON*.

When I joined *SHERATON* on 26 February 1991 there were only a handful of the once-119-strong class still in service. The ship was approaching 35 years old[5] and was in many ways an echo of a previous age. Designed to have a very low magnetic signature, the Ton class had a hull of double mahogany planking, teak decks and largely aluminium superstructure. Accommodation onboard for the sailors was at best at 1960s standards and yet the austere conditions seemed to encourage comradeship. Indeed, Ton crews were fiercely proud of their ships and disdainful of the new Hunt and Sandown class ships that were replacing them. The new ships were built of glass reinforced plastic to reduce their magnetic signature – the refrain from the messdeck being that they would rather be past it than plastic!

If my jobs so far had taught me how to handle ships at sea, in my new role I would learn a great deal about leadership, management and most importantly seamanship. Being second in command also gave me the opportunity to work closely with, and understudy, the captain, and in Lieutenant Richard Cunningham I was able to learn from the best. Richard was a gifted ship handler with a keen sense of fun, and an unflappable CO (Commanding Officer) who welcomed others' views and really cared about his officers and men – and he could not have been more supportive of his inexperienced XO and wardroom. Indeed, both the other officers were in their first jobs after training and did not have Officer of the Watch Certificates, but both were highly capable and responded extremely well to the trust that Richard put in them and in me.[6] The result was a really happy and efficient ship.

I joined the ship as she emerged from its final refit and, after trials and mine warfare operational sea training, we were loaned to the Fishery Protection Squadron. In every respect the ship excelled. For me SHERATON was first-class preparation for what might follow. I became skilled at running a minehunting operations room; at overseeing the challenging seamanship evolutions of streaming and recovering minesweeping gear; of launching and operating small boats; and above all else at judging the mood of a ship's company. I also greatly enjoyed conducting Fishery Inspection boardings which required a thorough knowledge of the law, people skills and, on more than the odd occasion, quick thinking. In all I conducted some 50 boardings with eight vessels subsequently being prosecuted for illegal activity.

Perhaps the most challenging boarding occurred on 19 January 1992, some 18 miles south of the Eddystone Light. We detected a large Danish commercial fishing boat called the ULLA MOLLER transiting through an area known as the mackerel box, in which it was illegal to catch that species. Richard sent the boarding party and me away, and having clambered onboard I made way to the bridge. On inspecting the boat's fishing log I saw that the skipper had failed to record where he had been fishing, and when asked to do so he indicated within the box. The team inspected the fish holds and discovered some 119 tonnes of mackerel carefully hidden under other types of fish. I informed the skipper that he was required to proceed to Falmouth for further investigation, and he simply increased speed and continued on his way to Denmark with SHERATON shadowing. It was now dark and the seas were far from calm, so what should I do? I told the team to make themselves comfortable since we were going to Denmark. The skipper certainly wasn't expecting this and asked what I was doing. I responded that the maximum fine for illegal fishing of mackerel was some £5,000 but the penalty for kidnapping an EU Fishery Officer was far more severe – it was his call. That evening we were alongside in Falmouth.[7]

As my time in *SHERATON* was drawing to a close my appointer phoned to discuss what came next – with a potential return to the original plan of navigating a frigate next. However, my experience in *SHERATON*, together with recommendations for small-ship command from both Andrew Dickson and Richard Cunningham, led me to rather cheekily suggest that I should command next. The appointer pointed out that it was unheard of for an officer without experience of navigating a frigate at sea to be given a small ship but he would put me forward for the autumn board. A few days later he phoned to say this would no longer be the case since I had been on that week's board and I was indeed to command a small ship next.

I took command of the P2000 class training ship HMS *PURSUER* on 22 April 1992. *PURSUER*, at 20m in length, was one of the smallest ships in the Fleet with the primary role of training cadets[8] from Sussex University Royal Naval Unit – which I also commanded. This arrangement had real advantages. It gave me valuable experience of dealing with shore authorities and the university, and more importantly enhanced my ability to exercise duty of care over the cadets since I trained them both ashore and at sea. The next 20 months were to be testing in a number of ways that I was not expecting. On joining, I told the ship's team that I thought this would be my only and last command – the Navy would not make the same mistake again! – and that I intended to get the most from it. Thus, we adopted a busy programme of being at sea on three weekends every month (Friday to Monday), and I would be at the university unit every Tuesday and Wednesday and take Thursday off. The only exception to this schedule was over the university Easter and summer vacations when we would deploy on longer voyages. It was a demanding schedule.

At sea it was quickly evident that as the only officer onboard I was the repository of bridge experience, but I was lucky to have a great team. My XO was the excellent Seaman Specialist Chief Petty Officer Pete Rosier,[9] who I had served with in *APOLLO*, a real character and a practical sailor. The marine engineer was the equally good Chief Petty Officer Derek Swords, the weapons engineer – although we had no weapons, he oversaw the radar and electronic systems – was 'Dick' Barton and the navigator's yeoman was 'Jacko' Jackson.[10] We would embark up to 12 midshipmen and usually one of three training officers from the URNU[11] – who I knew well and could trust to supervise on the bridge in my absence. My experience of delegating in *SHERATON* paid real dividends.

We sailed from Portsmouth on 4 July in company with HM Ships *PUNCHER*,[12] *BLAZER*[13] and *DASHER*[14] on the annual summer deployment which would see us circumnavigating the UK. After a brief visit to Faslane we were off the Isle of Arran on 10 July when what should have been a simple day of coastal navigation was interrupted by loud engine alarms. The port engine turbo blower had failed and burst into flames and the ship was quickly full of black smoke. I shut down both engines and mustered the midshipmen on the flying bridge – which being outside was clear of any smoke – and considered my options. The P2000s were in those days poorly placed for firefighting equipment. We had nine fire extinguishers and a solitary smoke mask which provided air to the wearer via a long hose which was held in the open air. The ship was fitted with a fixed firefighting system in the engine room which would inject BTM (Halon gas) into the space, removing any oxygen and extinguishing the fire. The problem was that this required the engines to be shut down and we were being blown by a fresh 20-knot-plus breeze towards the Isle of Arran. It seemed to me that the options were limited: fight the fire with what equipment we had, if that failed use BTM and accept the risk of being blown aground. In either case being forced to abandon the ship was a very real possibility.

As the enormity of the situation struck home, I became aware of the midshipmen all looking intently at me – I was the captain and I would know what to do. Thankfully my training kicked in – in my mind I was planning what to do at each stage of the process including distress calls and having to abandon ship, all the while retaining that naval trick of appearing in total control of the situation. At the same time Derek Swords, wearing the smoke mask, was fighting the fire with extinguishers being passed to him by Dick Barton whose protection was a damp tea towel. From my chair on the flying bridge I could see used extinguishers appearing on the upper deck, so I could count how many had been used – and see how near we were to the next step towards potentially grounding. The fire was extinguished with the very last extinguisher! We limped on our single engine towards Faslane, where we were met by a tug that enabled me to shut down the remaining engine and safely put us alongside. I don't think the midshipmen realised the danger we were potentially in, but the ship's company certainly did and there was a real sense of us (and me!) coming through a major test.

The postscript to this incident was that we conducted a ship's investigation into the fire which among other things recommended that Derek and Dick both be awarded commendations for their bravery and that the firefighting equipment in P2000s be increased. Unfortunately, the report went to the same organisation (indeed the engineering officer) who had endorsed the original firefighting outfit in the ships. He rejected all the recommendations, implying that the firefighting equipment was sufficient,[15] that we had been foolhardy in fighting the fire and that we should have immediately used BTM and accepted the risk of going aground. As the most junior commanding officer in the Fleet there are some battles that you simply can't fight – but I was sure we had acted correctly and was grateful for how my team had responded. So Derek and Dick had to put up with my – and the rest of the ship's company's – thanks and the very thoughtful message from HMS *DASHER*'s captain, Lieutenant James Morse, sent by light as we entered Faslane: "Well done the Engineers." Thankfully the damage to the port engine was minimal and thanks to the excellent support we received from Faslane Naval Base we were able to resume our around–UK voyage six days later.

If the 1992 summer deployment was eventful the following Easter one would be even more so. We sailed on 18 March from Portsmouth with our normal companions, *PUNCHER*, *BLAZER* and *DASHER*, which had a new captain in the form of Lieutenant Commander Gareth McHale. On 25 March *PURSUER* and *DASHER* left the other two ships and set out separately for Guernsey. As we approached Guernsey, I received a call for help from Gareth. One of his midshipmen had been taken ill and he was proceeding at full speed towards Guernsey to land her, when his port engine had failed. I was quickly alongside, embarked the now unconscious midshipman and proceeded at top speed to get her ashore. Having successfully done this and remembering the uneasy feeling of having only one engine, we returned to sea and escorted *DASHER* into St Peter Port.

The next day (26 March) we sailed for Jersey and the excitement really began when we became centre stage in an ongoing Anglo-French fishing dispute. The roots of this dispute lay in September 1992 when the EU had recognised a six-mile British limit for exclusive rights around the Islands. Until then there had been no restrictions on French trawlers in this area and they were not taking kindly to attempts to enforce the new regulations. We had only been at sea for a short while when we were contacted by the Guernsey Fishery Protection launch *PATRIOT* asking for assistance since two of their fishery officers, Steve Ozanne and Ben Remfrey, had effectively been abducted by the French fishing vessel *IMPATIENS*. The two fishery officers had boarded the fisherman on the Schole bank which is in Channel Island waters between Guernsey and Alderney. Having identified some infringements they directed the fishing boat to St Peter Port for further investigation, but the skipper ignored this request – in an echo of my own experience onboard the *ULLA MOLLER* some six months earlier. In this case, as Steve Ozanne later said to a reporter in the *Guernsey Evening Post*, the skipper 'didn't recognise our authority at all'. He contacted the nearby HMS *PURSUER* which quickly came to help, much to the relief of the two fisheries officers who did not know what to expect from their French hosts: 'We didn't know then than that we wouldn't be swimming.'[16]

The VHF radio call showed real concern for the safety of the fishery officers so I had no hesitation in offering what assistance I could and was quickly on the scene. What followed was largely an exercise in bluff conducted over the radio. *PURSUER*'s communication fit was, in terms of a warship, extremely modest and we were only equipped with a single VHF radio. I used this to establish comms with the Fishery Protection operations room in Rosyth – and they were able to keep the Fishery Protection staff, the Ministry of Agriculture and Fish and the Foreign and Commonwealth Office informed. Significantly, my conversations were not secure and the skipper of the *IMPATIENS* could overhear everything – from which it must have been clear that despite our size we were representing the UK government.

On our arrival *IMPATIENS* increased speed and headed as fast as it could towards French territorial waters – escorted by two other French fishing vessels. As the chase continued the fishery officers reported that threats were being made against them with knives. My objective was to ensure their safety and over the radio I requested, and gained, approval to board and seize the *IMPATIENS* if these threats continued. In reality such a move was out of the question – with a ship's company of four and 12 university students – but I was counting on the fact that the skipper would hear my request and take it seriously. He did, and all threats ceased. We stayed with *IMPATIENS* until it entered French territorial waters and the two officers were eventually recovered by a French maritime police boat.

With the incident over, *PURSUER* continued to St Malo for a planned two-day visit, but unbeknown to me the *IMPATIENS* episode had quickly begun to escalate. At 8am on the morning of 29 March a boarding team from HMS *BROCKLESBY* boarded the French trawler *LE CALYPSO* and, as in the *IMPATIENS* incident, ordered the boat to head for St Peter Port. *LE CALYPSO* ignored the instruction and headed instead for French territorial waters and Cherbourg where it landed the three British sailors. Unfortunately, while I was in St Malo my sister ship *BLAZER* (Lieutenant Commander Keith Creates) was in Cherbourg and as the Guernsey evening press reported, 'fishermen took revenge for the earlier boarding of *LE CALYPSO*. A mob of angry fishermen boarded the ship and dragged it from its moorings before they ringed the ship in mid harbour – *Le Calypso* was one of the vessels alongside *Blazer* stopping it leaving.'[17] Thankfully no one onboard *BLAZER* was injured but it must have been a frightening experience with at least one of the ship's company being threatened by a knife, the ship's Union Jack being burnt and for a while the ship being placed at risk of grounding.

It was around this moment that I phoned my wife Alison from St Malo expecting a usual catch-up call. She relayed the news from that evening's TV, that *BLAZER* was being attacked by French fishermen. I cut the call abruptly short, returned to the ship and sailed at the first opportunity for Guernsey. At this stage we had reports that the French fishing fleet were threatening to blockade St Peter Port and so I set off for there with the intention of escorting *DASHER* back to the mainland before the French arrived. I got to St Peter Port in good time and reported my intention of escorting *DASHER* to Flag Officer Plymouth[18] whose waters we were in and under whose orders I operated. The reply was not what I expected – the White Ensign was not going to be chased out of a British port by French fishermen. We were to stay put until the French departed.

Later that evening we were joined by *BLAZER* and shortly afterwards the French fishing fleet including my old friend *IMPATIENS* arrived and berthed astern of the three British warships. Overnight we planned for trouble: the upper deck was manned and we were prepared to prevent protesters coming onboard in a repeat of the Cherbourg incident. My night orders rather understated the situation:

> Overnight Quartermasters are to be particularly vigilant and report anything of concern to the Officer of the Day. Remember our friend IMPATIENS is in harbour. No unauthorised personnel are to gain admission to the ship.[19]

The next day the French fishermen departed and we continued with our training deployment. So ended perhaps the most unusual episode in my first sea command. A month later Steve Ozanne wrote to the Commander in Chief Home Command (Admiral Sir John Kerr KCB ADC) to place on record his thanks for *PURSUER*'s assistance. He wrote:

The officer's timely response to my request for help and his persistence in remaining with the French vessel undoubtedly helped to prevent the situation developing into one where either my boat crews or the boarding party were put in increased jeopardy. It was also extremely reassuring to see the white ensign alongside us…[20]

The Admiral's secretary forwarded Steve's letter with the brief add-on: 'You clearly handled a difficult situation with sensitivity and tact. Well done.'[21] In naval circles that is praise indeed!

I handed over *PURSUER* to its new captain[22] in November 1993 with a sense of a job well done and with the added confidence and self-belief that successful sea command gives. I was to take the next step in a warfare officer's career which was to specialise, and in my case I had chosen to become a Principal Warfare Officer (PWO) – responsible for fighting a destroyer or frigate on behalf of the commanding officer, and if needs be without them being in the operations room. What followed was a demanding 12-month course learning how to lead the operations team in defending the ship, and in my case becoming a specialist in anti-submarine warfare (ASW). The course consisted of a blend of theoretical and simulator work and two sea weeks – the first to test your ability to defend a ship against the full range of surface, air and sub-surface threats. The second, after your specialist or stream training, was spent conducting various anti-submarine exercises against a live submarine. Assuming these hurdles were passed the course would culminate in a test week of simulator training in which you would face high-intensity threats, and if you overcame them you would be a PWO. Passing was not a given and each PWO course consisted of about 16 students of which up to four might fail – and failure would mean the end of any realistic chance of further sea command and of promotion beyond commander.

MY PWO course did not start until June 1994 which gave me the time to prepare. In January I attended the Initial Staff Course at the Royal Naval College at Greenwich and after that, since I had not been in a destroyer or frigate for nearly four years, I was sent to the Type 23 frigate *ARGYLL* for some PWO refresher training. This was my first experience of the then-new Type 23 frigates and of a ship I would later get to know extremely well. It seemed to me that the real trick of leading an operations room is the ability not only to know your stuff but also to have the capacity to think, while taking charge of the operations room team (25 sailors or so) while looking at a computer display and listening to two radio circuits – one external and one internal – simultaneously! Unsurprisingly not everyone has this ability which explains why some fail the course. In *ARGYLL* I landed on my feet – we were conducting anti-submarine trials at the Atlantic Underseas Test and Evaluation Centre (AUTEC) off Andros Island in the Bahamas and the captain, Commander David Teer, showed huge trust in me by letting me run a number of exercises in the operations room in my own right. It proved to me that I had the ability to do the required mental gymnastics to be a PWO.

We were off Andros on 25 March and I was the on-watch PWO for a flying serial involving our Lynx helicopter. As the PWO I issued command intentions for the aircraft which on this occasion was to launch to conduct a flying display practice. The weather conditions were perfect, and a large number of the ship's company were on the upper deck to watch the display. The aircraft launched and early in its routine, at the end of what is known as a wing-over manoeuvre, without any warning on the radio circuit, it flew into the sea. Since the crash was near the ship we were able to quickly launch the seaboat and recover both the aircrew who were thankfully unharmed. This was an early and powerful lesson about the dangers of operating helicopters over the sea – a very experienced flight commander/pilot had, in perfect conditions, misjudged a manoeuvre but had managed to reduce the resulting unavoidable impact into the sea. Without this action we would have probably lost both men.

I joined HMS *DRYAD* for PWO training in June 1994 and a year later I emerged as a newly qualified warfare officer and was appointed to the Type 23 Frigate *MONMOUTH* as Principal Warfare Officer (Underwater) or PWO(U). I joined the ship in the Pacific halfway through a global deployment. My time in *MONMOUTH* is best described in two halves – the first in which I learnt my trade as a PWO(U) and the second in which I learnt about heading a department in a ship. In learning about ASW I was lucky to have Commander Al

Richards as my captain. A naval pilot who had flown ASW helicopters, he was a real enthusiast for the discipline, and the programme included a great deal of ASW activity including hunting for a Russian nuclear submarine in the eastern Atlantic. After a few months onboard I took over as the operations officer and head of the operations department. This meant not only heading the wider warfare department but also being responsible for the ship's programme – co-ordinating the various requests for activity from every department while ensuring that all mandatory activity was completed and the necessary sea areas and specialist support were arranged. This was particularly important after the ship emerged from a docking period and prepared for operational sea training requiring me to arrange post-upkeep sea trials (to check everything worked) and weapon training (to bring the team together for OST).

All was going well when I received an unexpected call from my appointer – he would like me to leave *MONMOUTH* before OST to go to London. At first, I was a little confused as to why he would move me to take a sideways step and join the frigate *LONDON* – but he quickly explained that he meant a high-profile staff job in the city of London rather than the ship. I was being asked to join the staff of Headquarters Director Special Forces (HQDSF) in London in a role that would expand my horizons. While this would be a great move for me the timing could not have been worse for *MONMOUTH*'s new captain. Commander Malcolm Sillars had relieved Al during the docking period and I was very much the continuity figure in the operations team; my early departure would mean that a relatively inexperienced PWO would have to step up as operations officer during OST which would test the ship and its new captain to the full. I remain grateful for Malcolm's support and his decision to let me move on to what was, without question, a great career move for me but a challenge for him – a sign of the unselfish nature of the man.

I was to spend over two years at HQDSF. This was a hugely rewarding appointment in which I gained my joint credentials – that is to say I worked closely with, and gained an understanding of, the Army and Royal Air Force. With a focus on operating in or from the sea my role also introduced me to amphibious operations which would be invaluable preparation for my later career. HQDSF was both an operational HQ for the UK Special Forces Group and an MOD Directorate, and so I was also fortunate to gain an early exposure to the workings of the Ministry of Defence and often represented the group at maritime planning and capability meetings. The role was both high profile and enjoyable and enabled me to gain valuable experience of how Defence – rather than a ship – worked. To my great surprise this tour came to an end in 1999 with my promotion to commander at the very young age of 32, and selection for the Joint Staff and Command Course followed by command of a frigate. And so I returned to *ARGYLL* but this time as the captain.

ARGYLL, like *MONMOUTH*, was a Type 23 frigate. At 133m in length it was over six times longer than *PURSUER* with a displacement of approaching 4,000 tons and a ship's company of 180 officers and sailors. The Type 23 was designed as an ASW platform with extremely quiet machinery and diesel electric propulsion to enhance its sonar performance. Should high speed be needed – rather than quietness – it was fitted with two gas turbines to drive it through the water. Equipped with both passive towed-array and hull-mounted sonar to detect submarines, the ASW weaponry included ship-launched ASW torpedoes and a Lynx helicopter equipped with torpedoes or depth charges. Despite its ASW roots the Type 23 is a multi-purpose fighting platform equipped with Harpoon anti-ship missiles, Sea Wolf surface-to-air missiles and a 4.5in gun for surface action or providing support to land forces. The Lynx helicopter was also capable of carrying a general-purpose machine gun or Sea Skua anti-ship missiles. And yet, returning to the fact that the Navy prepares its commanding officers very well for all that follows, I took command of *ARGYLL* in January 2001 with the benefits of a previous (albeit tiny) command and PWO training and roles that equipped me to fight the ship. And at this point I had had nearly 17 years of working with, and indeed leading, people.

ARGYLL was relatively fresh from refit[23] and so would be expected to be in operation throughout my tenure with a year of exercising around the UK followed by OST and an overseas deployment in 2002. I could not have hoped for a better programme – effectively a year to get to know the ship and prepare for the rigours of sea training with a focus on the deployment that would follow, which was programmed to be to the West Indies. We quickly got into the routine of exercise periods interspersed with week-long periods of providing training for student PWOs or navigating officers. With OST at the end of the year we practised our warfighting drills and effectively moulded the team that would deploy in the following year.

The highlight of the early part of the year was Area Capability Training (ACT) to practise and test our ability to locate, identify and track submarines using our passive sonar. We achieved this off north-east Scotland, operating with our sister ship HMS *NORTHUMBERLAND* against the nuclear submarine HMS *TRIUMPH*. In March we sailed to Brest to join a major Anglo-French exercise which provided excellent training in operating in a Task Group and enabled us to practise all our warfare skills. On Sunday 25 March we completed a surface warfare exercise and were heading to rendezvous with the French tanker *MARNE* to replenish when we lost power and a fire broke out in the forward electrical switchboard. The fire was quickly extinguished – with seven smoke inhalation casualties – but the ship was left with no electrical propulsion and no ability to go astern. There was no option but to head back to Plymouth on gas turbines for repair. On arrival, in echoes of *PURSUER's* entry into Faslane, we were eased alongside by tugs. I couldn't help but feel that we were very fortunate in that the fire had not broken out an hour or so later when the ship would have been refuelling from the *MARNE*. Loss of power when alongside the tanker would have been far more serious.

As we were programmed to deploy to the Caribbean one of our sister ships was due to go to the Gulf. A prerequisite of deploying into that theatre was a series of weapon trials including a successful Sea Wolf shoot, and by August it was becoming clear that equipment defects in the selected ship meant it was having difficulty achieving the required results. We were very much in the frame to step into its programme.

On every Tuesday afternoon off Plymouth, ships are put through their paces by Hawk jets simulating attacking aircraft. Tuesday 11 September was no different and I was at my console in the operations room as we manoeuvred against incoming raids. Just as a raid was approaching my excellent XO, Lieutenant Commander Kevin Fincher, appeared at my shoulder and said that the World Trade Centre was being attacked in New York. I initially dismissed this, saying that an exercise attack in New York was less pressing than the hostile aircraft currently approaching the ship. Kevin quickly explained that the New York attack was not an exercise – it was actually happening. To me this seemed like a pivotal moment in world affairs much like the fall of the Berlin Wall. The prospect of a possible Gulf deployment now certainly concentrated the mind and was confirmed during our operational sea training.

We deployed for the Gulf on 28 May 2002. Our primary role was to enforce UN sanctions[24] on Iraq by intercepting small craft attempting to smuggle valuable cargo (mainly oil and dates) out of Iraq to avoid the UN-controlled oil for food programme. This programme effectively permitted limited exports via established routes which ensured that any income would fund humanitarian aid. This involved positioning *ARGYLL* within Iraqi waters in the relatively shallow waters of the northern Arabian Gulf. Prospective smugglers would be located by radar and boarded by *ARGYLL's* team which included attached Royal Marines, and if either oil or dates were discovered they would be directed back to Iraq.

It was a clear mission – endorsed by the international community – which I had no difficulty selling to my ship's company. In the run-up to arriving in the Gulf I visited every messdeck and briefed everyone on our task and the international situation we were sailing into. This was reinforced by embarking Dr Saul Kelly – a lecturer on the Middle East – to brief on the regional issues before we arrived in theatre.

On 28 June we rendezvoused with our sister ship HMS *PORTLAND* (Commander Jonathan Handley) and took over from them the Gulf duty. That afternoon we met up with the tanker RFA *BAYLEAF* which was nominally part of my Task Unit and was commanded by the excellent Captain Shaun Jones. Shaun was one of the growing number of RFA captains who were also PWOs – and a real asset, combining considerable ship driving and warfare experience. Thereafter it was off to Bahrain for in-arrival briefings from UK and Coalition staffs.

This was a complex Coalition operation, occasionally involving mass breakouts of 15 or so dhows at night, which needed careful co-ordination with the naval units on the scene. The ships involved – with the necessary clearances to operate within Iraqi territorial waters – were *ARGYLL* and the Australian frigates *ARUNTA* (Commander Ray Griggs) and *MELBOURNE* (Captain Steve McDowell), with two of us usually being on station at any time. The ship first detecting the potential smugglers would become the on-scene commander and co-ordinate the ship's boarding teams. Command and control was made complex for me by two chains of command – Coalition and British. When conducting embargo ops my effective boss was Australian Captain Peter Sinclair, with the radio callsign X-ray Juliet, who in turn reported to the US rear admiral commanding the in-area Carrier Battle Group (CTF50). In parallel my UK boss was the UK Maritime Component Commander (UKMCC) – a commodore located at Bahrain – who in turn reported to the Permanent Joint Headquarters (PJHQ) at Northwood.

Our first day on task was 5 July when we conducted our first boarding on a dhow attempting to evade Coalition forces. This was successfully completed, and the dhow directed back to Iraq, when we received the urgent news that a Sea King helicopter that conducted routine stores trips around the Coalition force, known as the 'desert duck', had suffered a mechanical failure when landing on the destroyer USS *CUSHING*. The helicopter's tail rotor failed, sending the aircraft into a spin as it crashed onto the flight deck, went on its side and then slid into the sea. We stood by to send assistance, but it was a flat calm day and fortunately all seven onboard the helicopter were safely recovered. On 8 July we were sent into Iraqi territorial waters for the first time.

We were to conduct a further 113 boardings before we departed Iraqi territorial waters for the final time on 14 October, in the process discovering more than 10,500 tons of smuggled oil. It was not, however, straightforward. Being within the shallow Iraqi territorial waters presented navigational challenges, as did the adjacent Iranian waters and the occasional presence of Iranian patrol craft. There was always the uncertainty of what Saddam Hussein might do, noting that we were operating for long periods between 8 and 15nm (nautical miles) from CSSC-3 Seersucker anti-ship missile sites on the AL Faw peninsula, which if fired would give us 45 seconds to respond to an incoming missile.

In September things took a turn for the worse. The excellent XJ, Captain Peter Sinclair, with whom I had built a good relationship, was on leave and his place taken temporarily by a US Navy captain. On 2 September we boarded a dhow and discovered nothing but hay – not a high-value cargo and at this point not subject to sanction actions. As was the norm I informed XJ and said my intention was to allow the vessel to proceed. His response surprised me – we were to turn the dhow back to Iraq and thereby effectively impose a total blockade on Iraq which was certainly beyond my existing UK orders. I contacted UKMCC and PJHQ staff and they confirmed that I should ignore XJ's order and let the vessel continue on its way. XJ's very public response on the Task Group radio was that if I allowed the dhow to proceed, *ARGYLL* would be replaced by an Australian ship which would follow his orders. This was a real dilemma for me – and my ops room team. We understood our mission and its legal basis but also the importance of the Anglo-US Coalition. Should I do what PJHQ had told me to do and be ordered off station, or follow XJ's orders? In my mind I weighed the options with the fact that it was late at night so the 'A' team would not be on watch at PJHQ and the UK Commodore at UKMCC was himself unavailable. Despite my better judgement I sent the dhow back to Iraqi waters.

The next morning I spoke to UKMCC (Commodore David Snelson) and he supported my decision – and later PJHQ altered its direction and also supported it. It was clear that the pressure on Saddam was being increased and Anglo-US solidarity was the priority. Later that afternoon I flew to see the US naval captain (acting XJ) to ensure that he understood the nuances of my position and of commanding a Coalition Task Group. It was clear that he didn't, speaking of US plans, intentions, orders and rules of engagement (ROE), none of which applied to *ARGYLL*. It was an entirely amicable discussion, but the result was that on the following day his very impressive boss – Rear Admiral Stesky (CTF50) flew to see me and reassured me that he entirely trusted and valued the measured way that *ARGYLL* went about its business and we were his platform of choice to be up threat in difficult circumstances.

The international tension continued to rise. On 5 September two US F14 fighters overflew *ARGYLL* inside Iraqi territorial waters which caused some momentary concern since Iran also operated F14s. The next day an Iraqi surface-to-surface missile battery's radar came to life, resulting in us withdrawing 30nm to the south and it being destroyed by US naval aircraft on 7 September. Thereafter, we continued to operate as usual in Iraqi territorial waters but to me, at least, the nature of the operation had changed and there was a focus – certainly in US minds – on the forthcoming conflict. I was sure that the US were fixed on war, 10 days before President Bush addressed the United Nations General Assembly and warned Iraq that military action would be unavoidable if it did not comply with UN resolutions on disarmament and six months before the vote in Parliament enabling UK military action.

On 8 September the very real dangers of operating helicopters at sea were once again highlighted by a fatal crash. The US cruiser USS *MOBILE BAY* had launched its SH–60B Sea Hawk to film a routine boarding of a Syrian merchant ship. Unfortunately, while in the hover the helicopter's rotor blades struck the ship's masts and the aircraft crashed into the sea. The four US naval personnel onboard survived but an embarked civilian cameraman sadly died.

ARGYLL handed over its Gulf duties to HMS *CARDIFF* (Captain Tim Fraser) on 1 November and arrived back at Devonport on 28 November. My time in command was over and I left with a sense of a job well done and that the first stage of my career was over – I now had to prove myself in the world of policy and, in my mind, hopefully stake a claim for one more chance to return to sea.

CHAPTER TWO

Towards Bigger Things

I joined the Directorate of Naval Resources and Plans (DNRP) in London. The Directorate was responsible for overseeing the Navy's programme – that is to say ensuring that the Navy had been allocated sufficient resources to deliver its outputs and that these outputs were being delivered efficiently. Surprisingly the Directorate did not belong to the Navy but rather to the Defence staff under the umbrella of a rear admiral (Rear Admiral Rory MacLean) who oversaw the entire Defence programme. The Directorate was headed by Commodore Tim Laurence and was divided into two halves – the warfare shop headed by Captain Duncan Potts and later Mike Mansergh, who oversaw future equipment and ships entering service, and the programming shop headed by civil servant Tony Barbour and later Mike Davis who oversaw the use of resources. As the Plans desk officer I worked to Tony/Mike and was responsible for bringing together the two halves of the Directorate into a single naval programme and effectively co-ordinating the work of the strong team of 12 talented staff officers who worked there.

My time in DNRP was an education. I had the great benefit of working closely with Commodore Tim who was one of the most impressive MOD warriors that I have worked with, with the ability to quickly identify the solution to the most complex issues. As Plans I had to have a grasp of every aspect of the business and an in-depth understanding of where the resources and risks were. I also worked closely for the first time with, and for, civil servants and quickly appreciated the huge value they brought to Defence – not least in continuity and bringing diversity to an otherwise military team. My job also meant that I often briefed the First Sea Lord (Admiral Sir Alan West) and the Assistant Chief of the Naval Staff (Rear Admiral Tim McClement) on resource matters – and the position of the other Forces. Indeed, a key part of my role was working with my counterparts in the Defence, Army and RAF plans divisions to agree joined-up defence spending – and saving – plans. In this my joint experience at HQDSF paid real dividends and there was a real team spirit amongst the Services – which would contrast to what I would later experience immediately prior to the Libya campaign.

It was intellectually demanding work in a time – like most – when the defence budget was under significant strain, in this case with the additional burden of funding the ongoing operations in Iraq and Afghanistan. The Navy had to take its share of the pain and in 2003 a number of ships were placed in reduced support periods – when money was saved by simply not rectifying defects. The impact on both availability and the morale of the ships' companies involved was significant and it was obvious that this arrangement was not a long-term fix. The result, in 2004, was a series of significant defence cuts labelled Medium Term Work Strands (MTWS), the logic being that a smaller fleet that was properly supported would be far more effective. The RN was to lose three destroyers, three frigates, three minehunters employed as patrol craft and a nuclear-powered attack submarine. DNRP, and I, were at the heart of these difficult decisions and I was additionally responsible for preparing the material that was used to brief the Navy on the reasoning for, and the outcome of, the MTWS.

By December 2004 I was a seasoned MOD resource warrior in my own right having effectively co-ordinated DNRP business for two annual spending rounds. My reward was promotion to captain and an operational tour to Baghdad where I was to be the first senior advisor to the newly appointed head of the Iraqi Navy, Commodore Mohammed Jawad. I arrived in Iraq on 6 January and the following day made the journey from Basra to Baghdad. My task was effectively to help Commodore Mohammed establish a strategic naval staff and organisation within the MOD in Baghdad. This would mean shifting the centre of gravity of the Navy from the naval base in Um Qasar and establishing the right links with the various elements of the MOD. This was a significant challenge – when I arrived the Iraqi Navy had no office, furniture or staff in Baghdad – but it was satisfying work in which you could see rapid progress and it was a real pleasure to work for Commodore Mohammed. I use the term 'work for' carefully. Each of the senior Iraqis had Coalition advisors – mainly US, Australian or British – but many of these got the approach entirely wrong by trying to tell their Iraqi officer what to do and create a replica of their own national organisations. From the outset I made it clear to Mohammed that while I worked in Iraq he would be my boss and my loyalty would be only to him – in effect I would advise him as an Iraqi officer would do, doing what I thought was right for the Iraqi Navy. It worked well and we enjoyed an excellent professional relationship.

Together we had to navigate the politics of the Coalition and the Iraqi MOD. The division of effort was straightforward: I would look after the Coalition and advise Mohammed of what he had to achieve in the MOD. I probably had the easier task. The Coalition organisation, while complex, was unified in its purpose and my day-to-day work was within the Multi-National Security Transformation Command – Iraq (MNSTC-I). In terms of bosses I worked in parallel UK and a US structures. On the British side I was the maritime advisor to the Senior British Military Representative – Iraq (SBMRI), Lieutenant General John Kiszely, and my direct UK boss was MNSTC-I's Deputy Commander, the British Brigadier David Clements. MNSTC-I itself was commanded by Lieutenant General David Petraeus and mentoring and advising within the MOD was under the Australian Brigadier Ian Errington – my Coalition boss. A degree of my time was therefore spent ensuring that my Coalition, UK and Iraqi bosses were on the same page which actually was made easy by the quality and commitment of all involved.

I was also very fortunate to see David Petraeus in action. He was a deeply impressive officer who stood head and shoulders above the senior US officers around him. Partly because of his ability and very apparent drive but also his rank he was held in awe by his American staff who seldom – if ever – challenged him. This was most evident at the MNSTC-I evening command briefs where David Clements would invariably be the only person to offer an alternative view. On one evening I found myself as the only non-American officer in the briefing when Petraeus was being briefed on a plan which all, including him, seemed to agree – despite some obvious drawbacks. So I decided to follow Brigadier David's example and asked whether we were sure that this was the best course of action. For the American staff officers it was one thing to hear the general's thinking challenged by his British deputy but another to hear it being challenged a young Brit naval officer – this was after all largely a land campaign. The US staff looked uncomfortable, shuffled in their seats and remained silent, waiting to see how the general would react. Petraeus immediately got it, and not only thanked me for the constructive challenge – asking the team to think again – but then rather pointedly asked his US team why they never did the same. A real lesson to me on the need to welcome and encourage diversity of thought and challenge.

The Iraqi MOD reflected Iraqi/Arab culture – a fact that some advisors failed to get. Line diagrams, strategic plans and operating models, so beloved by Western ministries, gave way to personal fiefdoms and above all else the power of the senior commanders and ministers. I met and worked with them all. The most important was General Babakir Zebari, the Commanding General and Chief of Staff – effectively the Chief of Defence. Next was Lieutenant General Abadi, Babikir's deputy and head of joint operations. Commodore Jawad was the most junior of the service chiefs and there were countless Army generals in and around the MOD who, being senior to him, he found difficult, if not impossible, to challenge. Making progress was therefore a matter of currying favour and support from Abadi and, most importantly, Babikir. In this effort Jawad took his turn amongst a constant stream of officers lobbying for appointments, support and often finance. Under Jawad's direction I would prepare for him plans for naval structures, projects and expenditure and Jawad would choose the right moment or opportunity to make the case. He was more often than not successful – the lesson for me being that making these changes and winning support was subject to Iraqi niceties and timelines, not the strength of the argument. Put another way, culture trumps strategy every time.

All this was with a backdrop of Iraq and particularly Iraq in turmoil. The Coalition staff and the senior Iraqi leaders (including Jawad) lived in the green zone, protected by heavily armed checkpoints and concrete walls. Since I worked for a US command, I was accommodated in a complex of portacabins in the grounds of the former presidential palace. The green zone was mortared a number of times each week – and on a number of occasions the mortars landed far too close for comfort. Apart from this indirect fire the biggest threat to me was probably on the occasional visits to the red zone, often with Jawad, and the journey to Baghdad international airport – either by Puma helicopter or by road in UK Land Rover convoys down what was known as route Irish. On most days we received reports of – or heard – gunfire and explosions in the city.

However uncomfortable and indeed sometimes scary being mortared was, my experience in Baghdad led me above all else to really appreciate the bravery of the Iraqi people and in particular the Iraqi staff with whom I worked. They lived in the red zone where shootings and bombings were commonplace. They faced a daily threat of assassination or being caught up in a terror attack while they queued to get into the green zone, where they then faced the threat of mortaring with us. After a day's work they returned home to face it all again tomorrow. The first parliamentary elections since the 2003 invasion were held on 30 January – a momentous day which really underlined the commitment and bravery of the Iraqi people. A number of insurgent groups declared their intention to violently disrupt the elections and I wondered how successful they would be. At first my concerns deepened since, as I walked to the MOD that morning, I heard some very loud bangs as polling stations in the city were attacked. Despite over 20 being killed in Baghdad the turnout was far better than I and many expected, and the next day the pride of Iraqis when they showed the ink on their fingers – which proved that they had voted – was heartening. The losses of the day were nonetheless sobering – at least 44 killed in over 100 armed attacks, and the sacrifice of the Coalition was underlined by the shooting down of an RAF C130 which had taken off from Baghdad en route to Balad with the loss of 10 UK personnel. The price being paid was painfully high but the Iraqi people were unquestionably worthy of our support.

My six months passed quickly and on 12 July I set off to return to the UK, having handed over the senior advisor role to Captain Phil Buckley. It had been a challenging but rewarding six months and I had learnt a great deal about working in international and coalition settings – and, just as importantly, about myself. On reflection, I was struck by the fact that when the mortars were landing too close for comfort I thought not about the Iraqi Navy or my career but about what was really important – my family and friends. This may not be a surprising revelation, but it made clear to me what was really important in life and I think this realisation made me a more balanced and therefore effective leader thereafter.

On my return to the UK I joined the Fleet Headquarters in Portsmouth as the Fleet programmer[1] responsible for programming the Fleet's ships, submarines, aircraft and Marines. It was a hugely responsible role, my skilled team being responsible for the programme of Fleet units from six months out to two years in detail and beyond in outline. To do this I held the Fleet activity budget – in those days around £25M – and carefully juggled the Fleet's tasks (outputs) with maintenance and exercises and of course bids from individual units for tasking and visits.

On arrival I looked at how the Fleet generated ships with a new set of eyes. The process followed a well-established pattern that would see a ship emerge from refit or upkeep and then conduct safety training before sea trials. Once these were successfully completed the ship would officially join the Fleet for programming but before it could be tasked operationally it would undergo operational sea training and then take part in a Joint Maritime Course (Exercise) which was designed to prepare the ship for Task Group operations. The problem was that there could be a number of months between OST and JMC, meaning that the platform was not available to assist an already overstretched

Fleet. What is more, not every ship would be joining a Task Group and those that would often did not exercise and prepare with other units of their Group.

My team and I set about simplifying and accelerating the process to get ships available for tasking and bringing together and preparing Task Groups that would then deploy as a formation. Ships that would be deploying as singletons would not undergo JMC but deploy immediately (and TGs would form and undergo JMCs before deploying as a group). Having designed the new approach I had the not insignificant challenge of convincing the myriad stakeholders of the benefits it would achieve. Logic won the day and the result was more availability and better prepared and integrated Task Groups. To me the important lessons were the need to gain support, and wherever possible consensus, amongst stakeholders and that logic and the strength of your case can – if properly presented – deliver.

The next big issue that I tackled was the operational tasking of the Royal Marines. The Navy HQ fell into two distinct camps. The Amphibious planners wanted to hold the Royal Marine Brigade and the UK's amphibious capability at very high readiness for unforeseen contingent tasking. The problem was that the Army was becoming overstretched, supplying battalions to Iraq and Afghanistan and would welcome the Commando units taking their turn in the Operation Commitments Plot (OCP). To me the danger appeared to be of the Royal Marines (and our amphibious capability) being side-lined by not being part of Defence's main effort and my recommendation was that the Commando units should indeed take their turn in the OCP. The consequence would be a reduced amphibious capability. My recommendation was supported by the Deputy Commander in Chief Fleet,[2] with the Royal Marines going on to lead Operations *Herrick* 6 (October 2006–April 2007), *Herrick* 9 (November 2008–April 2009) and *Herrick* 14 (May–October 2011).

It was in this job that I had my first indication that all was not well with the relationship between the RAF and RN. At lower levels the relationship was good – in DNRP I had enjoyed good relations with my RAF counterparts; in *ARGYLL* we had an excellent affiliation with 47 Squadron; at Staff College there was real camaraderie between all three services and at DSF the RN/RAF had formed a happy and effective team supporting Special Forces. The friction appeared to be centred around Joint Force Harrier (JFH). Formed originally on 1 April 2000 as Joint Force 2000, it combined the Royal Navy's two Sea Harrier FA2 squadrons with the RAF's four Harrier GR7 squadrons. In 2006 the Sea Harriers were retired, and all the Joint Force was equipped with GR7 and GR9 Harriers. The force was designed to be able to operate from either land bases or the Invincible-class aircraft carriers, but there was a sense in some Fleet Air Arm quarters that the RAF – which commanded the force – underestimated both the value and the complexity of carrier-borne operations.

For me as the Fleet programmer the issue was the aircraft carriers' schedules. I had to keep the carriers' decks warm – that is to say the deck crews sufficiently experienced with fast jets to keep the ships at the Defence-directed required readiness for operations. Having worked closely with the Army Commitments teams on the OCP I fully understood the challenge my opposite RAF programmers had, since JFH was heavily committed to Afghanistan. To me it was an issue of making the right compromises to meet the Harrier Force's operational commitment and keep the carriers' decks in date for operations. I set out to help solve the problem and at a meeting at Air Command explained that I understood that preparing the squadrons for Afghanistan was the main effort, and to help I would position the carriers as close to the Harriers' UK operating bases as possible so that the ships could achieve the training they needed with minimal impact on JFH's schedule. Part of the problem in 2005 was that Harrier deployments to Afghanistan were four months long, meaning that the force was largely either deployed, preparing to deploy, or recovering from operations. We did achieve the minimum deck time and in subsequent years Harrier deployments to Afghanistan increased in length, creating a little more headroom. In the meantime, the lack of Harriers at sea was seen by some in the Navy as a sign of lack of commitment by the RAF and the maritime requirement as a complete distraction by some in the RAF. The seeds of potential disharmony were growing.

I expected to be the Fleet programmer for two years or so and had the additional joy of being selected to command at sea as a captain. However, after just under a year as the programmer I was contacted by the appointer who asked if I would like to be one of the two RN candidates to be the military assistant to the Vice Chief of Defence (VCDS). The Vice Chief was an army general and so the military assistant was either RN or RAF; both services put forward two candidates for interview. I think I was the RN's second choice since the other candidate was none other than my predecessor as Fleet programmer, Captain Clive Johnstone, who was currently in command of the assault ship HMS *BULWARK*. I approached the interview with the attitude that while I wouldn't get the job it was flattering to be put forward and good experience. I was therefore more than a little surprised to be selected – my sea command would be on hold.

I returned to the Ministry of Defence in December 2006 to take over from Duncan Potts as military assistant to both the Vice Chief and the Second Permanent Undersecretary (2nd PUS). The Vice Chief was General Sir Timothy Granville-Chapman who was a member of the Defence Management Board and the Chiefs of Staff Committee. Regularly deputising for the Chief of the Defence Staff, he effectively oversaw the central Defence staff and was the lead for joint service matters – such as education, doctrine and medical support. He shared the outer office with Sir Ian Andrews (2nd PUS) who often deputised for the PUS and effectively headed the civilian aspects of the central Defence staff. Ian was also a member of the Defence Management Board and interestingly sat on all three of the single Service Boards. The central staff was a combination of military and civilian personnel and the integrated outer office, together with the strong rapport between both men, resulted in joined-up and balanced leadership. Most impressively, neither had any single service bias or agenda and could be relied upon to do what was best for Defence.

For me this job provided a real insight into the higher management of Defence giving access, and often a supporting role, to the various meetings and discussions of the time. The big issue of the moment was the balance between the UK's military involvement in Iraq and

Afghanistan and the shift to Afghanistan becoming the main effort. A major initiative by General Tim was placing Afghanistan on a campaign footing and ensuring that the commanders in the field got all the support they needed from Defence and its joint organisations. Nowhere was his leadership more apparent than in the provision of protected vehicles, support helicopters and medical support – all of which General Tim drove forward.

If Defence had a main effort its chiefs of staff were far from a harmonious group with relations between the RAF and RN being particularly fraught. The friction remained around Joint Force Harrier with the RAF position being that there was no place in fixed-wing aviation for the Fleet Air Arm – and that it would be far more efficient for the Harrier force to be entirely RAF manned. In an attempt to resolve the issue two independent reviews of Joint Force Harrier manning were conducted and both supported the continued joint (RN and RAF) manning, but neither review was given the support they deserved by the RAF. In the middle of this the Vice Chief, supported by Sir Ian – through the single Service Boards – worked hard to ensure that this argument did not damage Defence and that the chiefs' relationships remained workable. Indeed, they deserve a great deal of credit for the fact that they did, their position always being one of getting the best for Defence through compromise and careful prioritisation. But despite this, the ill feeling between the RAF and RN staffs was palpable with both becoming increasingly paranoid about the actions of the other. Both spent a remarkable amount of energy and time studying naval Harrier pilot training pipelines in order to make the case for either its continuation or its demise – depending on the colour of their uniform.

I was to spend a hectic 23 months in the MA role, by the end of which my MOD credentials were strong. The Vice Chief's portfolio was so broad that I now understood how every area of the MOD main building worked and had seen the most senior officers and officials doing their business. Most importantly I had seen how Sir Tim's immense intellect and logic coupled with his consistently unbiased approach had delivered real progress for Defence. As my time was coming to an end the appointer brought me the news that I had been selected for promotion to commodore – but I think he was not surprised when I said that I would like to defer promotion in order to return to sea to command a large ship (the original plan). I felt that I had been away from the naval front line for too long and needed to be reacquainted with ships and sailors. A few weeks later the First Sea Lord, Admiral Sir Jonathan Band, asked me to join him on the steps of the main building – so he could smoke – and informed me that I was to command the assault ship HMS *ALBION* next. He said I would bring her out of refit and would learn a thing or two, and as usual he was not wrong.

I took command of *ALBION* on 29 April 2009. The 21,500 ton and 176m long assault ship was nearing the end of a prolonged period in dockyard hands and was sitting in the non-tidal basin in Devonport. We were due to commence sea trials in June with OST at the end of the year, with the ship becoming the Amphibious flagship in early 2010. For me, apart from getting to know the ship (how it handled) and its people, the task was to learn about amphibious operations and in 2010 how Task Groups functioned. Known as a Landing Platform Dock (LPD), the ship had two roles. The first, and most important, was to simultaneously support a one-star naval and one-star land commander – in naval parlance the Commander Amphibious Force (CAF) and Commander Landing Force (CLF). To do this the ship was equipped with a large operations room with the necessary communications and situational awareness to effectively host and support the integration of three commanders – myself, responsible for fighting and operating *ALBION*, Commodore Amphibious Task Group commanding the Task Group and Commander 3 Commando Brigade (3 Cdo Bde) who commanded the landing force. The ship also had a large Flag Planning space for the embarked staff to do their work and sufficient cabins and conference rooms for the embarked commanders. *ALBION*, and her sister *BULWARK*, were simply the best-designed and -equipped command platforms in the Fleet.

The ship's secondary role was to transport and land a force of between 250 and 600 Royal Marines utilising the ship's flight deck and landing craft. For this the ship carried four smaller Landing Craft Vehicle and Personnel (LCVP) able to carry 35 troops and two much larger Landing Craft Utility (LCU) able to carry up to 100 troops, one main battle tank or four lighter vehicles. The LCVPs were held in davits on the ship's upper deck while the LCUs sat in a the very large dock which opened to the sea via the ship's stern – effectively creating a harbour afloat.

Sitting as we were, not yet even in open water, the plan to regenerate the ship seemed clear to me: first we needed to get back to sea and prove that we could operate as a warship; then we needed to prove our ability to embark, support and land Marines; and then we would need to prove our ability to be a flagship supporting two Amphibious commanders and their staffs. Far from being daunted by this prospect it was a real delight to be able to take a platform from being a building site in dockyard hands and turn it into a flagship.

On 22 May we were finally out of the non-tidal basin and on 13 June we went to sea for the first time – to undertake sea safety training that would enable us to commence our sea trials programme. With three weeks of successful sea trials behind us the ship passed its Fleet Date Inspection on 21 July and the first stage of *ALBION*'s regeneration was complete – we were no longer a building site. Next came learning the skills of amphibious operations. *ALBION*'s ships company included its own Assault Squadron Royal Marines (ASRM) – headed by Lieutenant Colonel Richard Reardon who was both effectively the head of department and my amphibious advisor – and from whom I learnt a great deal. The ASRM were an integral part of *ALBION*, operating the landing craft and providing the interface with the embarked force. The successful amphibious ship driver needs to quickly understand that the main weapons system is the embarked force. For the ex-destroyer or frigate captain who is used to charging around the ocean testing weapons and sensors the pace of integrating the landing force into the ship and practising tactical embarkation and disembarkation (a series of exercises known as Wader) appears slow – but is nonetheless essential. Once mastered, the challenge becomes positioning the ship and its craft in the right place at the right time to enable the landing force to achieve both L (landing by helicopter) and H (landing by landing craft) hours. This requires a single-mindedness and a focus on the mission that I had not come across before.

The ship's ability to do this was fully tested by a two-part OST. Before Christmas the focus was on the ship and its amphibious systems and in 2010 we stepped up to commanding a small Task Group (*ALBION*, RFA *MOUNTS BAY* and HMS *LIVERPOOL*) and a larger embarked force (42 Commando) and some of the commodore's staff. In this later stage I effectively was the Commander Amphibious Force with CO 42 Cdo (Lieutenant Colonel Ewan Murchison) acting as the Commander Landing Force. The majority of my heads of department (logistics officer, marine engineering and weapon engineering officers) also joined the battle staff (as they would when the commodore embarked). As a result, I asked FOST (Flag Officer Sea Training) to give my second in command (Commander John Gardiner) and the Deputy Heads of Department experience in running *ALBION* – and they excelled. For me the value of the training and how far *ALBION* had come was demonstrated overnight on 23/24 January when we carried out our first full Commando unit insertion. A few hours into the exercise the Marines were involved in a live-fire incident ashore when live rounds were used instead of blanks. Thankfully no one was hurt but Ewan called and asked that since the exercise was effectively over ashore could 42 Cdo be re-embarked. With the minimum of fuss *ALBION* and its landing craft simply got on with the job and by the time FOST staff joined in the morning 42 Cdo were all back onboard having been fed and watered and their equipment stowed. *ALBION* was now an assault ship and the experience of leading a small Task Group was great preparation for my role supporting the commodore and the ship being the flagship.

The ship's first run out as the flagship was Exercise *Cold Response* in Norway. Commodore Paul Bennett (Commander Amphibious Task Group (COMATG)) and Brigadier Ed Davis (Commander 3 Cdo Bde) embarked in *ALBION* on 9 February – the Task Group consisting of HMS *OCEAN*, RFA *MOUNTS BAY* and HMNLS *Johan de WITT*. As flag captain (as I was known) my role was to be the commodore's deputy – commanding the TG when he was away from *ALBION* and being a sounding board during the exercise. In addition, I would get the TG in the right place at the right time to meet the commodore's intent and when needed (and asked by Commodore Paul) gently remind my fellow captains of the commodore's direction, enabling him to keep his powder dry. Paul was an excellent boss and although neither of us knew that I was effectively serving my apprenticeship for my own time as a TG commander, Paul was a great example to learn from. From the outset we had a very open and honest relationship, and he welcomed my views, even if they occasionally differed from his own and those of his staff – reinforcing the value of alternative perspectives and views in the command chain.

After *Cold Response* and a brief period in the UK the Amphibious Task Group (*ALBION, OCEAN*, RFA *LARGS BAY*) sailed for the eastern seaboard of the United States for a large exercise called *Auriga*. This brought us together with the Carrier Strike Group – commanded by Commodore Simon Ancona, Commander Carrier Strike Group (COMCSG) – in HMS *ARK ROYAL* supported by the Fleet support ship RFA *FORT VICTORIA* and HMS *LIVERPOOL* and HMS *SUTHERLAND*. It became quickly evident that the two Task Groups did not really need two separate one-star commanders and their battle staffs – and while we had too many commanders, we had too few destroyers and frigates to defend two separate groups. The tell-tale sign was that neither battle staff nor flag captain – myself in *ALBION* or Captain John Clink in *ARK ROYAL* – were kept busy looking after our respective TGs. In reality a single commodore could have commanded both. It is telling that the *Auriga* group would largely form what would become my Task Group off Libya.

ALBION returned to Devonport in August 2010 and I handed over the ship to Captain James Morley on 7 September. I thought that my seagoing career was over but I was ready for whatever came next.

CHAPTER THREE

Task Group

I was to be promoted to commodore and replace Commodore James Morse as Commander United Kingdom Task Group (COMUKTG). Despite the very impressive title, COMUKTG did not command a formed group of ships – rather I would be on call to command an ad hoc group of ships for a specific mission, and could expect to deploy for up to six months to the Gulf to command a group of Coalition ships. For the majority of my two-year appointment I would therefore be ashore at the Battle Staff Headquarters in Portsmouth and act as deputy to the admiral who headed the battle staffs and their lead on doctrine and procedures. The admiral was Rear Admiral Peter Hudson – a former COMATG who had been *ALBION*'s first commanding officer. The other one-star commanders I knew well – Simon Ancona (COMCSG) and Paul Bennett (COMATG). Compared to commanding either of the UK's formed Task Groups my role was – it seemed to me – the lesser one. In September and October my focus was getting to know how the wider Fleet battle staff worked and preparing for a Gulf deployment in 2011 prior to relieving James in November. This included attending the Maritime Component Commanders' Course in Bahrain.

Throughout this period the Armed Forces nervously awaited the outcome of the 2020 Strategic Defence and Security Review. Revealed by David Cameron on 19 October, the review was to have a major impact on the Royal Navy and my own immediate future. The review was clear: Afghanistan would remain the main effort for Defence and while delivering this commitment the pre-existing defence spending plans were unaffordable. Not only did the defence programme have a spending deficit of £38 billion over the next 10 years, but the country was also recovering from the 2010 market crash and Defence would have to play its part in reducing the national deficit to restore the economy. Some painful cuts were clearly inevitable.

For the Royal Navy the headline reduction was the decision to retire the existing carrier strike capability – with *ARK ROYAL* and Joint Force Harrier being deleted. In place of the Carrier and Amphibious Strike Groups would be a single Very High Readiness Maritime Task Force based around a reduced Commando Group Littoral Manoeuvre capability. This meant that the amphibious capability would be built around a fully supported Commando unit rather than the full Commando Brigade – meaning that only one of the two LPDs (*ALBION* or *BULWARK*) would be needed – the other being placed in reserve. The reduction in the scale of amphibious lift also meant that one of the four extremely useful *BAY* class LSDs (Landing Ship Docks) would be sold and with only one TG to protect the decision was also taken to reduce the frigate force by disposing of the last four Type 22 frigates.

Clearly the battle staff would need to be re-organised to reflect the new structure and the single maritime Task Group would need a commander. Admiral Peter was central to the thinking on this – his role would remain as the national deployable two-star Maritime Component Commander, and when it was the UK's turn the high readiness two-star NATO Maritime Commander. The RN Task Group would be commanded by a commodore and since I was the new kid on the block with recent TG experience, I was asked to take on the role. Admiral Peter organised a brainstorming meeting for all his one-star commanders and key staff and together we designed the new organisation. Simon Ancona was a real help and an invaluable source of advice as we enhanced the COMATG staff to enable it to carry out tasks that had previously been carried out by his team. COMATG would gain aviation, fixed-wing and targeting expertise. To strengthen its maritime warfare capability it would also gain a number of group warfare officers and a command-qualified submariner.

In terms of a name, since the TG would be at very high readiness (48 hours' notice to move) it formed part of Defence's new Responsive

Force and so we decided to call it the Response Force Task Group (RFTG). Its commander would (since I would command the UK's only maritime Task Group) retain the title of Commander UK Task Group (COMUKTG). In addition to commanding the RFTG I would also become the administrative authority for the Navy's largest ships – *ILLUSTRIOUS, OCEAN, BULWARK* and *ALBION* – meaning that I had to get to know them well enough to write the commanding officer's annual reports and to comment on the ships' heads of departments. The changes were rapid – *ARK ROYAL* paid off in December 2010 and I would relieve Paul Bennett as COMATG in January before rerolling both the COMATG staff and personally as COMUKTG on 1 February 2011.

My task was daunting enough without any operations – I had to establish a new organisation, a new brand and a new mindset. Admiral Peter could not have been more supportive or helpful. His message was clear: he expected me to be at the forefront of Task Group operations and his role was to provide any help I needed. As I arrived at the COMATG Headquarters at Stonehouse in Plymouth I felt as well prepared for the challenges as I could be.

I was supported by a strong well-formed staff that had spent much of 2010 at sea on amphibious exercises. I had five heads of department (HODs): the chief of staff (COS), and effectively my deputy, was Commander Tom Guy; Commander Richard Harris was my logistics lead; Lieutenant Colonel Al Livingstone RM was responsible for ISTAR (Intelligence, Surveillance, Target Acquisition and Reconnaissance); Lieutenant Colonel Paul Lynch RM was the lead for amphibious warfare, and Lieutenant Commander Tim Nield was the staff operations officer. Beneath the HODs was a newly enhanced staff of 31 officers and ratings bringing a real depth of planning ability and experience that would be tested in the months ahead. The original staff's experience lay fundamentally in amphibious operations and we needed to retain these skills to be able to plan and execute an assault up to 110nm from the ships. This included the simultaneous delivery of 1 Company Group by helicopter and 1 Company Group by landing craft and then the subsequent sustainment of combat operations by a Commando Group for up to 28 days.

For amphibious operations elements of 3 Cdo Bde would work with us – planning the landing forces' actions and effectively creating an integrated maritime/land staff. The relationship between me and the Commander Landing Force (CLF) was key and I was fortunate that for the next few months it would be Colonel Hayden White, the Deputy Brigade Commander. Whilst I commanded the Task Group we were co-equal for planning purposes and command of the landing force would transfer to Hayden once his forces had transitioned ashore – at which point I would go into the supporting role. The flagship was designed to support this key relationship – our cabins were adjacent to each other and we shared dining and briefing rooms. So we would spend a great deal of time together and I found Hayden to be a pragmatic and wise colleague who I could bounce ideas off. The brigade and the majority of its staff were in Afghanistan and so Hayden's team were very much ad hoc and were pulled together by Lieutenant Colonel Mike Roddy who was CO 539 Assault Squadron and Hayden's chief of staff.

The new COMUKTG staff needed to go beyond this and reconfigure, if needed, to conduct the full range of maritime operations including anti-submarine warfare and strike operations. Defence policy was clear that whilst the RFTG would be initially based around a Commando Group capability it would eventually include a Queen Elizabeth-class carrier-delivered carrier strike capability. Before then we might be called upon to deliver maritime strike – a combination of Marines, attack helicopters and submarine-launched Tomahawk land-attack missiles. This flexibility needed to be reflected in both the staff and the Task Group – so *OCEAN* might be a helicopter carrier for amphibious assault, anti-submarine operations or indeed attack helicopter missions. It seemed to me that the RFTG needed to offer the maximum choice through military options to the government. This was new thinking for some (both within and beyond the Navy) who thought in the outdated terms of the old Amphibious Task Group.

The first two months of the new COMUKTG's existence were busy building the new staff and its increased capabilities. In my first few days I hosted a TG seminar at which Commodore Richard Clapp and Major General Julian Thompson shared their experiences of the Falklands campaign with the staff. I spent time with my administrative boss (Rear Admiral Duncan Potts who had relieved Admiral Peter) and Rear Admiral Ian Corder, who as Commander Operations would be my immediate boss once deployed and on operations. My early focus was preparing for a three-month long deployment to the Mediterranean and Arabian Gulf, named Exercise *Cougar*, which contained two significant exercises. In Exercise *Albanian Lion* Admiral Duncan and his staff would validate my staff and I as being at the required capability standard. Then we would transit the Suez canal for Exercise *UAE Sea Khanjar* in which we would demonstrate our support of the UK's allies in the Gulf. We were due to sail on 26 April and return to Devonport on 8 August.

Before this COMUKTG and 3 Cdo Bde staff held Exercise *Green Alligator* embarked in *ALBION* alongside in Devonport in which Admiral Duncan's team helped me to practise our planning procedures. This was invaluable since the battle staffs integrated into the flagship and proved that we could generate a variety of options and plans – under pressure. As well as exercise planning we were also planning the *Cougar* deployment for which I had been given a number of objectives in addition to validating the staff: work up and validate 40 Commando as the Lead Commando Group; further Anglo-French integration; demonstrate a Simple Intervention Capability – or the ability to conduct non-combatant evacuation operations; and conduct strategic wider regional engagement. COMUKTG's staff had plenty to do.

I spent a great deal of time getting to know the various personalities with whom I would work and of course those in my team. The *Cougar* group would include the Type 23 frigate HMS *SUTHERLAND* (Commander Roger Readwin) and the Type 42 destroyer HMS *LIVERPOOL* (Commander Colin Williams). I met both and visited *LIVERPOOL* in Portsmouth harbour. I also visited 40 Cdo which would be a key element of the deployment and met its impressive commanding officer, Lieutenant Colonel Matt Jackson. Since furthering Anglo-French integration was one of my objectives, I had a very useful telephone conversation with my French opposite number Rear Admiral Phillipe Coindreau. We immediately hit it off – he was clearly a man to do business with and would be deployed in the Mediterranean with the French Task Group based on the aircraft carrier *CHARLES DE GAULLE* at the same time as us. He welcomed the idea of working together – including allocating a French ship to the UK TG. This was to be the start of a key relationship.

There were also the ships that I had administrative responsibility for to consider. HMS *OCEAN* was preparing for operational sea training and would – if things went well – be ready to sail with us on 26 April. The ship had a number of significant material defects and many thought that achieving the deployment start date would be a challenge but its highly capable captain, Captain Keith Blount – had my full confidence and he assured me that they would be ready to go. *BULWARK* was preparing to take over from its sister *ALBION* as the high-readiness LPD at the end of the year and I managed to embark in March for a visit to Den Helder for discussions with my Dutch opposite number Commodore Peter Lenselink. This enabled me to get to know Captain Alex Burton and his team and also to strengthen the UK/NL Amphibious Group concept for which I was the nominated commander. We would also be taking some Dutch Marines on the *Cougar* deployment. The final big ship was HMS *ILLUSTRIOUS* – at that stage in refit in Rosyth preparing to relieve *OCEAN* as the amphibious helicopter carrier in late 2011. I managed to visit it in the dockyard where it was in the capable hands of its executive officer (Commander Jason Scott) since the captain (Jerry Kydd) had yet to join. I did manage to get a feel for the ship, its senior team and the challenges they faced in returning *ILLUSTRIOUS* to sea and into the assault ship role.

As could be expected from a battle staff, comprehensive plans for the deployment were quickly worked up. Sailing ahead of the group would be our submarine HMS *TRIUMPH* which would act as an enemy submarine attempting to prevent our passage into the Mediterranean. To counter this threat, ASW Merlin helicopters would be embarked in the aviation support ship *ARGUS* which with the remainder of the group (*ALBION, OCEAN, MOUNTS BAY, CARDIGAN BAY, LIVERPOOL, SUTHERLAND, FORT ROSALIE*) would hone its ASW skills. HMS *OCEAN* was due to embark British Army Apache attack helicopters and conduct live hellfire firings early in the deployment. Once into the Mediterranean the focus would be reacquainting 40 Cdo with amphibious operations – they had recently returned from Afghanistan and had not been to sea for over 18 months, so much of May would be spent conducting Wader drills as 40 Cdo became familiar with tactical loads and offloads by helicopter and landing craft. This would culminate with the high-profile Exercise *Albanian Lion* on 27 May – 3 June. Thereafter the group would transit through Suez for the UAE exercise (2–8 July) before returning to Devonport.

As comprehensive and good as the *Cougar* plan was it was becoming very evident that real-world events were going to impact heavily on the Task Group's plans. Just as COMUKTG was formed the Arab Spring was erupting in North Africa. In Tunisia protests overwhelmed the

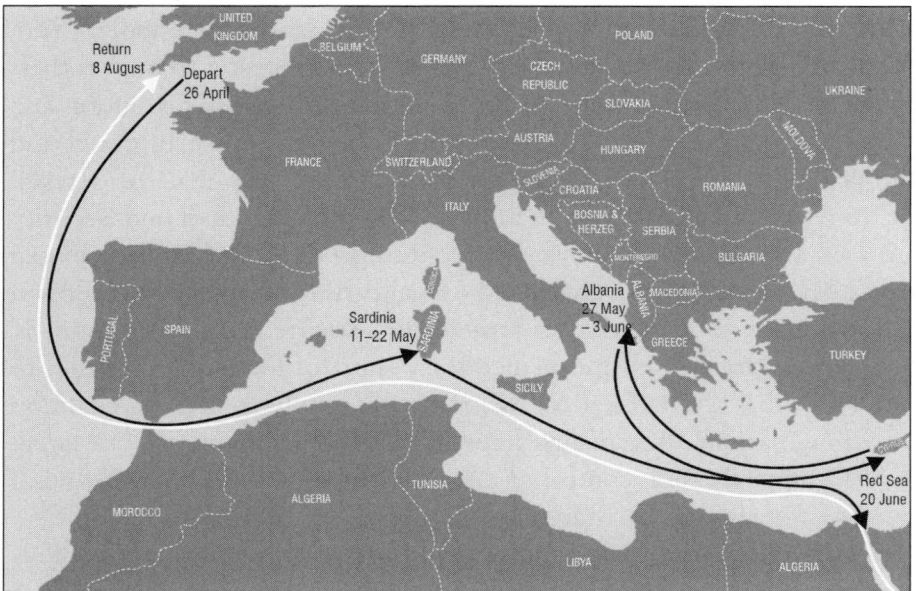

Operation *Cougar*

country's security forces and on 14 January the country's president, Zone al-Abidine Ben Ali, was forced to step down and flee the country. This brought massive crowds into the streets in Cairo and on 11 February President Mubarak left office. In Libya 17 February was declared a day of anger with protests erupting in Benghazi, Derna, Bayda, Ajdabiya, and Zintan – although the capital Tripoli remained largely calm. A number of cities in the east of the country declared their independence and Gaddafi forces began to attempt to put down the revolt. Gaddafi air strikes were evident around Brega and on 24 February regime forces attacked Az-Zawiyah. A conflict had begun. On 26 February the United Nations Security Council passed resolution 1970. Drafted by France and the UK, it called on the Libyan government to end the violence immediately and imposed an arms embargo. By March the apparent success of the popular movements in Tunisia and Egypt also led to unrest and instability in Yemen, Bahrain and Syria.

Although the protesters in Libya had made early gains they were in most cases lightly armed civilians who were poorly placed to oppose Gaddafi forces who quickly made ground, recapturing a number of rebel cities. On 13 March Gaddafi's son, Seif-al-Islam, said on Libyan state radio: 'You, the armed gangs, listen to this very carefully and repeat it to our brothers in the east. We are coming.' At this point the fate of the revolution and the civilians who supported it appeared to be very much in doubt and the possibility of a massacre of civilians seemed very real. As a result on 16 March France, Lebanon and the UK proposed a second Security Council Resolution on Libya. The resulting UNSCR 1973 was passed on 17 March and effectively gave the legal basis for military intervention in Libya since it demanded an immediate ceasefire, established a no-fly zone and authorised all means necessary short of foreign occupation to protect civilians. The French – who initially sought to create a coalition of willing nations – began air strikes against Gaddafi forces on 19 March. NATO officially took control of the arms embargo on 23 March and of the air campaign on 31 March.

An exercise period was rapidly turning into an operational deployment. In the Ministry of Defence a Strategic Middle East North Africa

(MENA) estimate was undertaken by the commitments (operations) staff for the RFTG which concluded that:

> The strategic MENA Estimate, conducted in light of the current wave of instability across the MENA region, identified the need for strategic rebalancing. It recommended the early deployment of the RFTG to mitigate NEO response risks, and other contingent tasking in the MENA region. Sec Pol and Ops view is that early deployment would meet the strategic imperative to remain balanced, provide strategic messaging towards OP ELLAMY's embargo strand, and be prepared to respond to short notice contingencies.

The Deputy Chief of Defence Staff (Military Strategy and Operations), Lieutenant General Simon Mayall, directed:

> To provide the opportunity for early deployment of the full RFTG, fast passage and early Suez transit in order to give maximum flexibility in response to the ongoing situation in Libya or other crises in the MENA region and to ensure that maximum benefit is gained from the RFTG's deployment.
>
> That the readiness of the RFTG and supporting elements should be; reduced to R2 (48 hours notice) as soon as possible, be prepared for a 6 month deployment and be prepared to transit into the Gulf at short notice if required. Furthermore, a RFTG Vanguard be placed on orders to sail no earlier than D+12 (5 Apr 11) to poise in the central/eastern Mediterranean.
>
> If not sailed before, the remainder of the RFTG should sail as planned on 26 Apr 11 to join the lead element in the Mediterranean, where they are to continue the planned COUGAR Scheme of Manoeuvre i.e. to develop and confirm contingent capability to Bespoke Intervention standard and contribute to operations and influence in the ME JOA.

I now had the go-ahead to begin planning a very different deployment. The original Task Group was already being depleted – HMS *TRIUMPH* sailed to the Mediterranean to provide a Tomahawk firing option and HMS *LIVERPOOL* sailed to be available to assist NATO enforcing embargo operations on Libya. The final early departure was RFA *ARGUS* that deployed to provide options off Yemen. This left me focusing on General Simon's direction to prepare an RFTG Vanguard that might sail on 5 April, that is to say, three weeks earlier than planned.

Commander in Chief Fleet's staff tasked me to conduct an estimate on what we might need and what we might do on deploying. To help, Tom (my chief of staff) and I together with the nucleus of our planning staff shifted from our base in Plymouth to the Fleet Headquarters in Portsmouth. This enabled us to have easy access to the Fleet's commanders, programmers and importantly the new Maritime Intelligence Fusion Centre located at HMS *COLLINGWOOD* which helped us build an intelligence picture of the region. At this stage we needed to be broad in our geographic thinking – our orders were to provide options in response to the situation in Libya, and other crises in the region, so Syria and Yemen both featured in our planning. Early thinking suggested that our most likely roles might be in evacuating entitled civilians/UK personnel out of a crisis area, enforcing the arms embargo or delivering humanitarian aid.

I enjoyed the intellectual 'so whatting' that this planning stimu-lated – it was an exhilarating but at times frustrating process. To my staff and me it seemed that we were very likely to be deploying on an unscripted and reactive deployment – a first in our careers – at the centre of world events. It would also be a valuable opportunity to demonstrate the value of the RFTG and indeed the Royal Navy after the Strategic Defence and Security Review. Some of the Fleet staff could not cope with this move away from planned exercises and activity – they really believed that *Cougar* would proceed as originally planned since their schedules said so.

The first friction point was the composition of the vanguard. To me the driver was to deploy with the maximum capability to offer potential choice to the government. This meant *ALBION, CARDIGAN BAY* (with *MOUNTS BAY* close behind), *SUTHERLAND* and 40 Cdo. *OCEAN* had not completed OST and so would not be able to sail before the original 26 April date. The missing part was logistical support. RFA *FORT ROSALIE* was due to sail on *Cougar* and our planning quickly identified that it would be key in sustaining the vanguard. Not only was it the group's store ship, it also carried key stores and munitions for 40 Cdo and had airborne early warning Sea Kings embarked that would provide much-needed situational awareness around the group. I was more than a little surprised to be told by the Fleet programmers (noting that it used to be my shop) that it could not sail early since it was needed to be the big ship around which others would exercise in a long-planned exercise off of Scotland. I lost the argument… for now.

The next sticking point was over when the group might deploy. Some traditionalists within Fleet argued that although the individual ships in the groups had been worked up at FOST the Group itself had not. As result they argued that before heading to the Mediterranean we should spend a period working up in home waters. My view was that the RFTG was declared to Defence at Very High Readiness (48 hours' notice to move) – a point emphasised in General Simon's orders – and when ordered to go we should proceed as quickly as possible to the arc of crisis. After all, I could integrate the force as we moved to the Mediterranean and FOST staff could always forward deploy to assist with training. The quicker we were in the Med the quicker we could offer options to the government. This argument – lost on some of the middle management – was immediately supported by the Commander-in-Chief Fleet Admiral Sir Trevor Soar and his deputy (Vice Admiral George Zambellas) who saw the strategic and political import of the RN being seen to react quickly if needed.

The plans were in place, and we now waited for the order to sail – or not. From mid-March we were on and off the bus – even as we approached the potential 5 April earliest sailing date. On Thursday 31 March I was at home in Sussex, in the barber's chair, when my work mobile rang. It was Commander Operations. We were to sail on 7 April – not only was *Cougar* beginning early, it was no longer an exercise deployment but an operation. Operation *Cougar* was on.

CHAPTER FOUR

Operation *Cougar*

The decision to sail was in many ways a relief – we at least had certainty on going. Although ordered to sail by the MOD we would remain under Commander in Chief Fleet's command and my immediate boss would be Rear Admiral Ian Corder (Commander Operations) at Northwood. Admiral Ian issued his orders to me on 31 March:

> COMUKTG is to execute the deployment of a RFTG for up to 6 months, in the Mediterranean and East of Suez, in order to provide options for response to the ongoing situation in Libya or other crises in the MENA region, develop and demonstrate a RFTG capability by Dec 11 and exploit the utility of maritime power in support of wider Defence objectives.

We were to be prepared to conduct, on order:

> Evacuation Operations
> Humanitarian Assistance
> Maritime Security Operations
> Embargo
> Protection of Maritime Infrastructure
> Amphibious Assault
> Strike
> Wider Regional Engagement

On 5 April I had dinner with three of my key commanding officers – Captain James Morley (*ALBION*), Commander Roger Readwin (*SUTHERLAND*) and Captain Andrew Betton (*OCEAN*). Captain Andrew had yet to take command of *OCEAN* and would do so as it finished sea training – just as they sailed to join the group. I didn't underestimate the challenge he would face in getting his ship through work-up and then focused on operations and this was

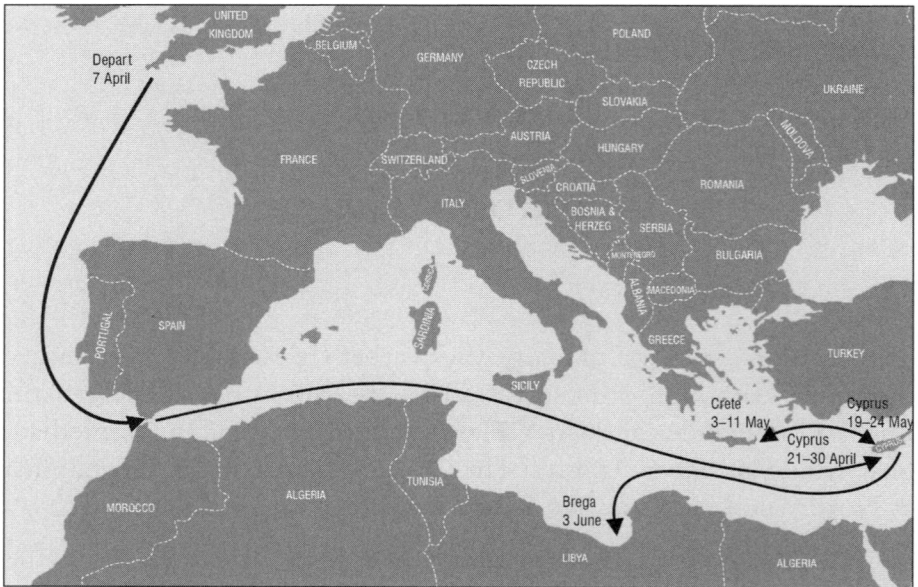

Operation *Cougar* actual RFTG movement

a good opportunity to introduce him to *Cougar* and the team. My message at this dinner and at the pre-sailing conference in *ALBION* the next day was clear – we were sailing on a key operation to offer the widest possible choice to the government against a wide range of contingencies. I couldn't say what our scheme of manoeuvre or tasking might be and even when we might return to the UK – dealing with that uncertainty whilst maintaining our ability to act would be our challenge. At the conference Roger Readwin and James Morley were joined by the other commanders, Colonel Hayden White (Commander Landing Force), Captain Paul Minter (*CARDIGAN BAY*) and Matt Jackson (40 Cdo) and their senior teams. It was clear that that I had an impressively strong and highly capable command team who were ready for all that might follow.

The Task Group got underway on 7 April and headed into the South-West Approaches. The day began with a very early interview with Radio Devon enabling me to explain that we were deploying in order to offer the widest range of options in light of the developing and potential crisis. The deployment also marked an important first for the RN in that it was the first Task Group deployment to include an enhanced intelligence fusing capability – consisting of equipment and specialists – based on that developed ashore in Afghanistan. This gave me much greater situational awareness than I had ever seen at sea before and it paid dividends almost immediately. At the very first evening's briefing, intelligence drew my attention to Libya and specifically the deteriorating situation in Misrata. While the rebels were strongest in the east of the country they also held some key locations in the west including the country's third largest city Misrata, which includes a major harbour – providing a source of humanitarian supplies, and escape for the encircled population. Reports indicated that thousands of refugees were in a small area by the harbour which, together with the city centre, was under indiscriminate rocket, gun and mortar attack. Getting supplies into, and evacuees out of Misrata was becoming essential. I discussed the intelligence picture with Admiral Ian's team in Northwood and was shortly afterward tasked to plan to support the delivery of humanitarian aid into the city by using the landing force to secure port infrastructure. We were asked to provide a proactive screen to port infrastructure – shipping to escort merchant ships in and out with close air support from the French carrier *CHARLES DE GAULLE* which had arrived in the central Med on 22 March.

The staff worked up options all day on 8 April and back-briefed Hayden and me on the following day. While the planning revealed that we could conduct the mission it also revealed a number of key limitations. Firstly, the absence of *OCEAN* and its air group meant that any landing would need to be done by landing craft. Secondly, while an administrative offload was entirely possible 40 Cdo were not yet familiar with *ALBION* and *CARDIGAN BAY*'s procedures and landing craft and were therefore unable to conduct a tactical landing and in a number of cases had not zeroed their weapons. Finally, should the landing force become involved in high-intensity fighting (which was much more than the level of activity being proposed) we would need the munitions and stores in *FORT ROSALIE* still conducting an exercise off of Scotland. I signalled what we could do – and equally the limits of our capability – to Northwood, where our advice was well received, and we were put on notice for potential tasking in Misrata.

The Misrata planning had also helped to clarify my priorities – we needed to work up 40 Cdo as quickly as possible for tactical insertion and a first step would be zeroing weapons in Gibraltar where we arrived on Monday 11 April. Also alongside was the Type 22 frigate HMS *CUMBERLAND* commanded by the impressive Captain Steve Dainton who had been operating off of the Libyan coast with HMS *WESTMINSTER*. It is a good naval tradition that when in harbour ship's captains call on each other – and on the senior officer afloat – not only to exchange niceties but also to share their views and experiences of where they are operating. Steve's visit to the flagship was particularly valuable since on 24 February he had gone alongside a number of times in Libya's second city of Benghazi and evacuated 454 people including 129 British citizens. A week later the destroyer HMS *YORK*, which had been on its way to the South Atlantic, was diverted to both deliver medical supplies and evacuate eligible personnel from Benghazi to Malta. Meanwhile *CUMBERLAND* was attached to NATO forces enforcing the arms embargo on Libya until relieved by *LIVERPOOL*. After Gibraltar it would be returning to Devonport to pay off as one of the SDSR reductions. Speaking with Steve therefore gave me real insights to potential evacuation operations in Libya and the challenges of operating off the Libyan coast.

Warships normally run to a ship's programme that identifies days at sea and planned port visits. These visits are planed months in advance in order to gain the necessary diplomatic permissions needed for warships to enter foreign waters. While I had clear objectives and priorities, the Group's movements were in advance of the planned *Cougar* deployment and we simply had no diplomatic clearances in place for anywhere! So instead of a programme I introduced decision points. Put simply, I would offer a range of options to Fleet Staff for where we might go and what we might do next, and a date at which I would need their decision taken. The first was set for 14 April – did we proceed to Misrata or continue to build our capability? My recommendation if we were to do the latter was to proceed to Cyprus since it had a

British Sovereign Base Area which, like Gibraltar, included a UK air and logistics hub. It also had some good areas for amphibious training for the group and 40 Cdo. On 12 April the Commander in Chief Fleet (Admiral Sir Trevor Soar) visited the flagship and we briefed him on our plans to build our capability and to continue to offer choice to him and the government – an approach he thoroughly endorsed. We would sail for Cyprus.

At about the same time I received tasking to provide potential options to place psychological pressure on the Gaddafi regime. The resulting ideas ranged from siting the Task Group off Libya, inviting the press to witness amphibious training at Cyprus or simply releasing a press release. The result was a press release and an interesting interview with the local press.[1] The rather gratifying headline of 'Task Force Ready for Action' appeared. In the interview I denied a *Sunday Times* report that we would sail to deliver food and medical supplies to rebel-held cities with the Marines providing protection on the ground (which sounded uncannily like our Misrata planning!) but stressed that we were about providing military and political choice to our government, and that our tasking would depend on real-world events. This coupled with the psychological tasking enabled me to think about the importance of the effect we could have on the Gaddafi regime through a combination of physical action (such as positioning as well as intervention) and the clever use of the media.

The group sailed from Gibraltar on 14 April with me hosted in *SUTHERLAND* by Roger Readwin overnight. Building on my experiences of the importance of briefing the mission in *ARGYLL* I visited all of Roger's messdecks and spoke to as many of his people as I could. My key messages were around the political and operational importance of our deployment, the need to deal with uncertainty, and the nature of our potential tasks – including UNSCR 1970 and 1973. *SUTHERLAND* was an extremely friendly and well-run ship and my words were well received by all onboard. Roger had an excellent way with his sailors who were clearly galvanised by his very evident enthusiasm and clear passion for the Navy, his ship and warfare. Roger was the sort of captain you would want to face danger with and a real asset to the Group. My only slight concern was the number of material defects that *SUTHERLAND* had; in particular the 4.5in gun was defective and we were to spend a great deal of time and external expertise getting it back on line. I asked Roger to keep an eye on his defect list since I might need a fully capable escort – fairly soon!

On return to *ALBION* I made two important phone calls. The first was to the Commander British Forces Cyprus (CBF Cyprus), Air Vice Marshall Graham Stacey. I asked for his help in working up the Task Group's amphibious capability in his area – a really can-do officer, he could not have offered more support. It was clear that the Cyprus option would work well. My next call was to make first contact with the NATO maritime command structure off Libya. This was with two main objectives – to make the connection to NATO in case my group would work with them and to check that all was well with *LIVERPOOL* which, although originally one of my ships, was now working as part of the NATO Group. The NATO Maritime Component Commander (Admiral Ian Corder's equivalent) was the Italian Vice Admiral Rinaldo Veri located at the Allied Maritime Command Headquarters at Naples. The NATO TG Commander and my equivalent at sea was Rear Admiral Filippo Foffi who flew his flag in the aircraft carrier *GARIBALDI*. I was very fortunate that Admiral Veri's chief of staff was the British Rear Admiral Jon Westbrook – and it was with Admiral Jon that I made contact. Like Graham Stacey, the Admiral was hugely helpful and supportive. He explained that NATO airstrikes were not at that stage having a decisive effect due to restrictive collateral damage rules and that maritime forces faced a real challenge due to a lack of fuel tankers amongst the allocated NATO forces. He was to provide a most useful link into NATO maritime thinking.

As we passaged towards Cyprus my main effort was to get key messages around the group and I took the opportunity to stay overnight in RFA *CARDIGAN BAY* where I was impressed by both Captain Paul Minter and his team and the embarked 40 Cdo. Paul, like most Royal Fleet Auxiliary Captains, had huge experience of sea command and, since he was an Amphibious ship driver, of amphibious operations. It was clear that *CARDIGAN BAY* knew and were good at their business and that I was fortunate to have another sage captain in the group. I was particularly pleased to see how upbeat 40 Cdo were – despite losing their Easter leave. I spoke to the Commandos as a group and at the end of my remarks asked if there were any questions. One Royal Marine asked whether, now that it was Operation rather than Exercise *Cougar* they would receive operational allowance. I replied that having just come from Afghanistan they knew that operational allowance was a reflection of the risk and strain of operations, and that in *CARDIGAN BAY* the only risk was too much good food. He answered, 'Fair one sir but I had to ask' – to the amusement of the unit. Their can-do attitude and warm acceptance of my key messages – including the mission and uncertainty – were a real reflection on Lieutenant Colonel Matt's outstanding leadership.

On 15 April regime pressure on Misrata reached a new high with heavy fighting breaking out as regime troops and tanks entered the city. We were once again put on notice to head to Misrata – which was seriously considered by London until 19 April, by which time the rebels were able to stabilise their positions – assisted by NATO air strikes. On the 18th two civilian vessels were able to enter Misrata and evacuate 600 people from the city and although the situation remained perilous, we were able to continue to Cyprus.

On 21 April we arrived off Cyprus and went straight into Exercise *Cypriot Wader* amphibious drills with 40 Cdo practising their skills, embarking into landing craft and inserting tactically from the sea. This was planned to culminate in a test exercise on 27 April when the landing force would be tactically landed ashore. My staff focused on three issues: would the Task Group be able to remain on station until October; thereafter how could ships and staff be relieved to extend the RN presence beyond October; and, perhaps most pressingly, what should our immediate scheme of manoeuvre be after Wader drills were complete? The answer to this last question was shaped by real-world events. The initial focus was Syria where, since March, protests against the Assad regime had been nationwide. In April the Syrian government had increased their military operations to suppress the uprising and on 25 April, as we were practising our amphibious skills only 210nm west of Syria, they began a major assault against rebels in the city of Daraa. The violent way in which the Syrian forces suppressed the uprising sent shock waves through the diplomatic community and called into question the safety of European and UK nationals in the country. We were asked to submit options for the RFTG to conduct non-combatant evacuations from Syria – which we duly sent to Northwood on 25 April. Once again our capability was limited but at least my landing force was now ready to insert tactically from the shipping and when *OCEAN* joined us – in two weeks' time – we could provide helicopter lift as well.

In Yemen popular protests against President Ali Abdullah Saleh had continued throughout March and April and although the president agreed to the Gulf Co-operation Council producing a transition plan, he still clung to power. As a result, the situation deteriorated and since early April RFA *ARGUS* and RFA *FORT VICTORIA* had been in the region with elements of 40 Cdo to provide an evacuation capability. We were tasked to be prepared to offer assistance and reinforcement. As a result, we were now effectively at 48 hours' notice to conduct operations off Misrata (Operation *Ellamy*), or to be off Yemen (Operation *Hunt*) or Syria (Operation *Hythe*). The simple method of speed/time/distance and a chart indicated that we should operate in the area of water between Crete and Cyprus. We had a plan.

The week of 25 April saw the remainder of the Task Group departing the UK. HMS *OCEAN* (with its new captain), the stores ship RFA *FORT ROSALIE* (Captain Ross Ferris) and the tanker RFA *WAVE KNIGHT* (Captain Vernon Ramsey-Smith) all departed the UK and would markedly increase our capability to launch and sustain operations. I updated both RFA captains by phone as they set out to join us. The 26 April was an important day for the Group. We were visited by the Chief of Joint Operations (CJO), Air Marshal Sir Stuart Peach. I knew him from my time as the MA to VCDS when Sir Stuart had been the Chief of Defence Intelligence and it was a real pleasure to host him in *ALBION*. The visit was key since, in my view, we really shouldn't have been under Fleet's command but CJO's – any operation we might conduct would be joint by nature. In terms of my role this would change very little since Rear Admiral Ian Corder would remain the UK Maritime Component Commander but in effect it would for the Task Group change Ian's boss from Admiral Soar to Sir Stuart. I explained this to CJO and briefed him on the range of options we had worked up for various contingencies. He was very receptive to all he heard and, as he left, he urged me to keep it up and be ready for anything – he was sure the Task Group would be used. Sir Stuart was accompanied by CBF Cyprus – Air Marshall Graham – who remained as upbeat and supportive as ever.

The next decision point for Northwood was 30 April when the options were: proceed east of Suez to be in place for operations off Yemen; remain poised in the eastern Mediterranean for either Syria or Libya; or head west to join *OCEAN* in the eastern Mediterranean and begin the planned Exercise *Cougar* programme with amphibious training off Sardinia. Loitering in the eastern Mediterranean made the greatest operational sense and this was my recommendation which was supported by Fleet. *OCEAN* would rendezvous with us in a week's time in Crete. Thereafter we would return to Cyprus for further training and to integrate the new arrivals into the Group – while staying in the optimum area to respond to any of the potential operations. As we approached Crete yet another potential task emerged for the team to plan – in this case using the landing forces boat group – provided by 539 Assault Group Royal Marines – to interdict the inshore maritime traffic Gaddafi was using to supply his forces. As was becoming the norm the plan was submitted to Northwood where it joined the now growing list of potential RFTG tasks.

ALBION went alongside in Souda Bay, Crete on 3 May. Seven valuable days would be spent in harbour, waiting for *OCEAN* and the new joiners to arrive. Having all of the amphibious shipping in one place would enable us to reconfigure our stores and equipment around the shipping and also to give the vanguard ships and 40 Cdo some rest and recreation – effectively their first since Devonport a month earlier. *OCEAN* arrived in the adjacent berth on 8 May and did not make an auspicious start. That evening some of the ship's company decided to celebrate their first run ashore since completing operational work-up by going to town in Chania town centre – their behaviour was not good and out of step with the remainder of the Task Group who were already very much in an operational mindset and were pacing themselves for a very long and demanding deployment. The police were involved but thankfully the situation was well handled by them and the more sober of *OCEAN*'s team. The next day Captain Andrew came to see me and tried to pass on the reports that he had received that the trouble ashore had been caused by other ships of the group. Unfortunately for him, at the time I had been on the opposite side of the harbour having a quiet meal on the waterfront and had witnessed the whole thing so I knew exactly where the troublemakers had come from!

On 9 May I also took the chance to visit the nuclear submarine *TRIUMPH* that had originally been part of the group but had deployed early to support the Libya operation. *TRIUMPH* had already been in the thick of things – firing Tomahawk Land Attack Missiles (TLAM) into Libya on the 10, 19 and 24 March. In early April it had briefly been relieved by its sister *TURBULENT* and had returned to Devonport but was now back on task. I was hosted by the impressive and able commanding officer Commander Rob Dunn who was able to brief me on submarine operations close into the Libyan shore and the nature of Libyan and particularly Gaddafi's inshore traffic. Suffice to say that the coalition submarines were doing a remarkable job providing situational awareness of the coastal region.

The next day turned out to be telling for the Task Group's future. In the morning Hayden White and I hosted a COs' forum in the flagship. The team was now complete with a number of notable additions. The flag captain and Commanding Officers HMS *ALBION* (James Morley), *OCEAN* (Andrew Betton) and *CARDIGAN BAY* (Paul Minter) were joined by Peter Farmer (*MOUNTS BAY*) and Roger Readwin (*SUTHERLAND*) and the captain of the small French frigate *COMMANDANT BIROT* (Commander Thibault de Possesse), whose ship was now under my command. On the land side Matt Jackson (40 Cdo) and Hayden's chief of staff (Mike Roddy) were there. With *OCEAN*'s arrival I also now had a much enhanced air group of Army Apache attack, Sea King 4 troop carrying, Sea King Mk7 airborne surveillance and control, and Lynx Mk7 utility helicopters. The Tailored Air Group – as it was known – was commanded by Commander Jol Woodard supported by Commander Paul Morris who was Commander Helicopter Forces representative in the planning staff. From my staff Tom Guy (Chief of Staff) and David Bruce (Policy Advisor) were present and I was pleased that both Jerry Kydd (*ILLUSTRIOUS*) and Alex Burton (*BULWARK*) were both able to attend since both their ships were regenerating after refit and I wanted them to prepare their ships for potentially taking the places of *OCEAN* and *ALBION* in the autumn. This was an important opportunity to welcome the newcomers to the group and to update them on the variety of potential tasks that we might be called upon to undertake. It had been decided that we would transfer to CJO's command on 18 May and it seemed to me that some form of operation was very likely – the message being build capability quickly and be ready for anything.

On 10 May the French flagship *CHARLES DE GAULLE* was also alongside in Crete and that afternoon I paid my first face-to-face visit to Rear Admiral Philippe Coindreau. He was as engaging as ever and it was clear that President Sarkozy was being extremely forward-leaning on Libya and wanted to be seen to take decisive action. The Admiral echoed Jon Westbrook's earlier comments about the difficulty of achieving the required precision from fast jets alone and said that he thought there was a real opportunity to use his group's fixed-wing aircraft in conjunction with attack helicopters to successfully strike Gaddafi forces threatening civilians in Libya. I took this as signalling to the UK that France wanted co-ordinated action and that attack helicopters were becoming part of their plan. Admiral Phillipe and I agreed that we would work closely together – if we were deployed on the same mission – and he assured me that FNS *COMMANDANT BIROT* was now fully part of my Group. On return to *ALBION* I signalled the French intent and their desire to work with us to Northwood.

The now much larger Task Group sailed for Cyprus on 11 May. We had decided to integrate the group and prepare 40 Cdo for helicopter insertion in an exercise called *Cypriot Lion* which would complete on 24 May. To assist me Fleet had arranged for significant support from Flag Officer sea training (FOST) back in the UK – including forward deployment of Hawk jets to simulate air and missile threat and a number of training teams to assist individual ships. Commander Steve Holt from Admiral Duncan Potts' battle staff also brought a small team to validate the combined COMUKTG and 3 Cdo team. While *Cypriot Lion* would prove excellent training for the units of the group the planning staff had to keep a very close eye on real-life events which took precedence with all three scenarios – Libya, Syria and Yemen – remaining entirely possible. On the next day as the Task Group went into a complicated series of replenishments at sea we received orders to scope the feasibility of conducting amphibious landings at Brega in eastern Libya, with the French providing close air support from *CHARLES DE GAULLE*. This was not doable without significant risk – advice that I passed back to Northwood, Admiral Ian Corder telling me that a series of Anglo-French meetings were planned for the weekend culminating in a National Security Council on Monday 13 May.

On Sunday I visited FNS *COMMANDANT BIROT* and was impressed by the can-do attitude of the captain, Commander Thibault. At only 1,351 tons, 80m long and with a ship's company of around 100, the 27-year-old frigate was less capable than *SUTHERLAND* but its inclusion in the RFTG was an important statement of French commitment to working with the UK. The impressive captain was certainly very clear that he was delighted to be part of the group and he would undertake any mission I gave him. The next day was a change of scale when I visited the helicopter carrier *OCEAN*. At 22,107 tons it was the largest warship in the Royal Navy and a ship I knew reasonably well, having visited it in build when I was a lieutenant commander at HQDSF and having worked with it a great deal when I drove *ALBION*. The new captain, Andrew Betton, fitted in well with the strong group of TG commanding officers – energetic and forward-leaning with a very nice way with his team. The challenge he initially faced was one of the mindset of his people. During my visit a number of his team – of all ranks – asked when *OCEAN* would be home. When I said plan on the end of the year, I was met with incredulity: I must be wrong – the ship was only programmed to be away for a month! I wasn't surprised since I knew the effort the ship's company had made to get the ship through operational sea training during which they had seen a six-week training exercise in the Mediterranean as the end prize. I tried hard to dispel this view and I know Andrew did too, but the events of the next few weeks would eventually do this for us.

The Group chopped operational command from CINCFLEET to CJO at midnight on 17 May and with this came a range of Libya planning tasks – from potential amphibious operations to continued contribution to the information campaign – for Operation *Ellamy*, as UK operations in Libya were called. There were also the first questions about working with the French and specifically the use of attack helicopters (AH). With the change of command came some new relationships for me to develop. My direct boss remained Admiral Ian Corder and his excellent deputy Captain Paul Abraham – with whom I would be in almost daily contact in the days ahead. The most significant change was that CJO was my new two–up, and I would need to work closely with his staff so that I could understand Air Marshal Stuart's intent. At the forefront of CJO's staff was Major General Gordon Messenger, CJO's Chief of Staff (Operations). Thankfully since General Gordon was a Royal Marine our paths had crossed a few times – most recently when we had served together in the MOD when I was the MA to VCDS. On the very first day under CJO's command I made a number of phone calls to contacts at CJO's headquarters (the Permanent Joint Headquarters) including to General Gordon. It was a good call. General Gordon was upbeat and reassuring as always and I was pleased that I had a friendly voice and supporter within PJHQ – as events turned out I would need him.

On 19 May I welcomed CINCFLEET, Admiral Sir Trevor, back to the Group. In 24 hours he received countless briefings, observed

Cypriot Lion, visited most of the ships and had lunch with the TG's commanding officers. As he departed, CJO's standing one-star commander – Brigadier Richard Felton (known as Commander Joint Force Operations) – joined for a brief visit. Richard was very focused on potential evacuation operations in Yemen (Operation *Hunt*) where we still had 80 Royal Marines at readiness in RFA *FORT VICTORIA*. It was a good opportunity to compare notes and to demonstrate to him the capability of the Group and more specifically the ability of HMS *ALBION* to support two one-star commanders and their staffs. As *Cypriot Lion* drew to a close we approached the next decision point for PJHQ (for the first time rather than Fleet). The options were: did we remain in the eastern Mediterranean in readiness for any task; did we proceed east of Suez for potential operations off Yemen; did we continue to Exercise *Albanian Lion*, or finally did we proceed to Libya and Operation *Ellamy*? To me the mood music seemed to be pushing us increasingly towards Libya and the potential use of AH had continued building momentum since that initial conversation with Admiral Coindreau in Crete. It was rapidly developing into a real possibility.

On 20 May I decided that we should focus on preparing for potential Libyan operations and I would send a small amphibious force to support *Albanian Lion* while the majority of the ships would remain in the vicinity of Cyprus awaiting the call. So, on 24 May *CARDIGAN* and *MOUNTS BAY* with 40 Cdo detached and headed for Albania. By then I was very aware of high-level Anglo-French talks that increasingly pointed towards AH strikes. I was aided massively in my situational awareness by both official channels – Paul Abraham at Northwood did a first-class job at keeping me in the picture – and also by my policy advisor, David Bruce. David would be a key asset and friend in the weeks ahead because he brought an unmilitary perspective to my planning team – and was always quick to offer constructive challenge. I was reminded of my time on General Petraeus' staff when David said, 'Commodore, are you sure you want to do that?' or 'Have you considered the following?' It sometimes meant we had got it wrong and always that we should at least think again. David also had another key strength. He was an experienced and streetwise civil servant with great contacts in Whitehall – and that meant that I got read-outs of security council and ministerial meetings much faster than would otherwise be the case. On the day that the *BAYS* left us I therefore heard that the Prime Minister and President Sarkozy had agreed that both British and French attack helicopters would be used in the strike role.

CHAPTER FIVE

Maritime Strike – The Early Strikes

Although we had not yet received orders the political news and direction of travel was clear, reinforced by the media. A *Times* Paris reporter wrote on 24 May:

> Britain is sending ground-attack helicopters to Libya in an attempt to break the stalemate between rebels and forces loyal to Colonel Muammar Gaddafi. The escalation in UK involvement in the NATO offensive will involve 4 Apache helicopters arriving in Libyan waters onboard HMS OCEAN towards the end of the week.

While at this stage the UK Ministry of Defence did not confirm the decision, the Armed Forces Minister telling Parliament that no decision had been made, the French Foreign Minister Alain Juppé was reported as saying, 'What we want is to better tailor our ability to strike on the ground with ways that allow more accurate hits. That is the goal of deploying helicopters.'[1] The French were clearly setting the pace.

The *Times* reported on 25 May that 'Britain is already believed to be sending four attack helicopters on board HMS *OCEAN*' and that they would arrive by the end of the week (27 May). The journalist Tom Coghlan added that 'Britain is taking a calculated risk in deploying attack helicopters in Libya, because their crews will be facing one of the world's most advanced air-defence missiles (SA24)'.[2] The *Times* was right about the missile threat but not our arrival time off Libya. The French were putting pressure on the UK government for us to start strike missions as quickly as possible – a message passed to me by PJHQ, but my aircrew, ships and staff needed to be properly prepared and I resisted the pressure to begin straight away. Attack helicopters had traditionally been used to provide close air support of land forces – to launch them on strike missions from the sea was an entirely new proposition. They had never flown operationally from ships at night and Libya was still in many ways an unknown. I spoke to my aviation team and the Apache lead in *OCEAN* and decided that we should spend at least three days conducting mission rehearsals in Cyprus and let the staff 'so what' the various missions and implications. I reassured the aircrew that I would only declare the Group ready for action when all their preparations were complete, a message I passed back to Northwood. With passage time it meant that, if ordered, we would be ready to go around 3 June.

Our preparation began in earnest on 26 May with Exercise *Cypriot Eagle*. In the flagship the staff held a number of aviation forums where we discovered from our aviation advisors all we could about operating Apaches and then considered all the tactical implications of launching them into Libya. Understanding the capabilities and limitations of Apaches would be key and I was fortunate at this point to welcome Lieutenant Colonel Jason Etherington to my staff. Jason was the commanding officer of 4 Regiment Army Air Corps (AAC) from where our Apaches from 656 Squadron were drawn, and he happened to be visiting his people when I needed his expertise most. It was a mark of the man that he realised that he had a key role to play advising me and my staff, so he stepped away from the day-to-day running of the Apaches and became an absolutely vital member of my team. An early conclusion was the closer to the sea that the targets were the better, since being able to strike feet wet (over the sea) would mean avoiding flying over enemy territory with a missile and MANPAD (man-portable air defence system) threat.

On the 26th I also managed to pay a brief visit to *FORT ROSALIE*, the stores support ship that would play such an important part in supporting the Group in the weeks ahead. It is often said that you can quickly sense the feel of a ship, and I know from my various visits that this is true. *FORT ROSALIE* was a focused, effective and welcoming ship, reflecting its captain, Ross Ferris – he would prove to be a key member of the command team.

The Apache aircrew commenced intensive preparations for what was to come under the careful guidance of Major Will Laidlaw, the Officer Commanding (OC) 656 Squadron AAC. Thankfully they had practised firing Hellfire missiles off Gibraltar and this continued against floating targets; missile and 30mm gun firings were conducted by day and night. To test the aircraft's ability to detect fire control radars and the pilots' ability to take evading action all the Apaches flew against *OCEAN*'s Phalanx close-in weapons system radars – with the reassuring outcome that when locked up by the Phalanx's radar the aircraft systems gave the required warning and the pilots were able to evade. The aircrew also had the not insignificant challenge of tactically launching and recovering to *OCEAN* at night. This required them to get airborne and then drop to 100ft in formation and approach a hostile shoreline, complete the strike and return to a fully darkened and radio and radar silent ship. On the nights of 27 and 28 May we tried to replicate conditions in Libya within the Sovereign Base Area of Cyprus. Areas of pro-Gaddafi and contested terrain were created and the aircraft tasked with a deliberate (pre-planned) strike on three pro-Gaddafi technicals – the term used for a gun mounted on a flat-back civilian vehicle. The aircraft would have to practise the ingress and egress and the transition from low flying over the sea to over the land. Once at the target the scenario was such that some regime forces would drop their weapons and flee to test that the aircrew fully understood their Rules of Engagement (ROE) – which precluded attacking those not threatening civilians or their own aircraft. The Apaches would then return to *OCEAN* and wait on deck alert for a time-sensitive opportunity target which again they would launch and strike.

While the Apaches would launch from HMS *OCEAN*, I would command from HMS *ALBION* with *SUTHERLAND* and *COMMANDANT BIROT* providing force protection. A Sea King Airborne Surveillance and Control helicopter or SKASAC would provide airborne command and control (C2) and area overwatch/early warning. Off Libya itself we expected the strike to be supported by a much larger air package provided by the air component in order to supply on-call support if needed. To simulate this I used the Air Force officer on my staff, Flight Lieutenant Woody Wood, to replicate the various air communications on the required circuits. The two nights went well and after the final Apache had been recovered and Will had debriefed his crews he called me to say that his teams were good to go.

The staff meanwhile went into the 'so whats' of the expected tasking. It was quickly evident that our four Apaches – even together with French AH – would not have a decisive impact on the ongoing struggle in Libya; after all considerable numbers of fast jets were already committed to protecting civilians. But psychologically the threat of Apaches striking with great precision at night could be great, and might curb the excesses of Gaddafi forces. To counter this the loss of British aircraft and personnel could have the reverse impact and greatly damage the coalition. To me it seemed that my key consideration should be to reduce the risk – as far as possible – to the Apache crews. My experience – not least the loss of two US helicopters in daylight and in benign conditions in the Gulf – reinforced the risky nature of flying over the sea, even without engaging and being engaged by the enemy.

The position of the ships when launching Apache strikes would be a key consideration – informed by two important factors. Firstly, in the unlikely event that the aircraft suffered a generator failure its flying instruments would be illuminated by battery – with a finite life which corresponded to a flying range. In addition, I was keenly aware that the Apache was designed for land operations and had poor buoyancy – if one ditched it would sink extremely quickly. Recovering the aircrew was further complicated by the fact that I had no helicopters in the force that could hover at night and therefore winch up survivors. Recovering aircrew – if they had managed to get out of a sinking airframe – would therefore depend on boats sent from the ships. I had to reduce the time the Apaches spent transiting over the sea and the resulting calculation was that we should position some 20nm off the coast. When you added to this the anti-aircraft capability of Gaddafi's forces which, as the *Times* had said, included the latest MANPADs and radar-controlled guns, I was aware of the very real risks we were running.

The staff and I also pored over a number of key documents. There were both UNSCR 1970 and 1973, as well as a UK Ministerial Submission in which outlined the levels of risk that were acceptable for HM Forces. Added to these were the UK Rules of Engagement and a similar NATO profile and finally the targeting directive which listed what could and, as importantly, what could not be struck. It also included details of what weapon systems had sufficient accuracy and reduced collateral damage to strike certain targets.

The possibility of impending action and our accessible location off Cyprus attracted some high-level visitors. Admiral Duncan Potts arrived to witness one evening of *Cypriot Lion* and was extremely supportive and encouraging, passing his confidence in me back to the Fleet HQ. He was closely followed by General Sir Nick Parker (Commander in Chief Land Forces) accompanied by Air Vice Marshall Carl Dixon (Commander Joint Helicopter Command). 656 Squadron Army Air Corps was Army manned and part of the Joint Helicopter Command – with some Navy exchange pilots – and supported by REME ground crew so their visit focused very much on the Apache teams.

On 28 May we received the long-awaited orders from PJHQ, CJO's intent being that 'the RFTG is to deliver Attack Helicopter FIRES in the Libyan littoral in Associated Support to NATO's Operation Unified Protector.' Detailed planning got underway.

The wording of CJO's orders contained the important phrase that we were in 'associated support' to NATO. This introduced a very complex command and control structure into which I had to fit. The Task Group remained under UK command, the chain being CJO to Admiral Corder in Northwood, then to me in the TG and then from me to allocated units and squadrons. In military speak CJO had Operational Command (OPCOM), Admiral Corder had Operational Control (OPCON), I had tactical command (TACOM) and the unit commanders had Tactical Control (TACON). The complexity lay in the fact that when attack helicopters launched for strikes in Libya they would effectively chop to NATO command.

The NATO headquarters was located in Naples where the American Admiral Sam Lockear wore two hats: he was both Commander of

NATO's Allied Joint Forces Command and Commander US Naval Forces Europe. This meant that early on in the Libyan crisis he had overseen US naval operations off Libya but as the US decided to let the other NATO nations take the lead he handed over command of Libya operations to his Canadian deputy, Lieutenant General Charles Bourchard, who became the NATO Joint Commander. Thankfully for the UK, and particularly for me, his deputy was Rear Admiral Russ Harding – a former commanding officer of HMS *OCEAN* who understood my business and would be a great point of contact for me in the weeks ahead.

The NATO Air Component Commander was the American Lieutenant General Ralph Joddice located in Izmir, Turkey, although the NATO air campaign was planned and managed from the Combined Air Operations Cell (CAOC) in Poggio Renatico near Bologna in Italy. The CAOC would generate the Air Tasking Order which would allocate missions for Apache strikes – and to be effective we would need to ensure that AH expertise was correctly represented in a largely fixed-wing-based headquarters. Lieutenant Colonel Jack Davis had been deployed from the UK to establish an AH planning cell and as we headed for Libya I was able to send my Apache planning officer in *ALBION*, Major Chris James, to join Jack. Chris had been involved in the staff planning onboard and crucially understood the complexities of operating from the sea and knew the key squadron and staff personalities well. He would be joined in the CAOC by Commander Simon Wallace who provided dark blue expertise. The relationship with the CAOC AH cell and my staff targeter, Lieutenant Emma Ward, and Apache teams would be key – taking potential targets and identifying which were suitable for Apache strikes and getting them into the Air Tasking Order. The senior Brit in the CAOC was Air Commodore Ed Stringer who, as the British red card holder for NATO missions, could veto UK participation in individual strikes and would effectively also ensure we had suitable targets. Once authority for a mission was given by the CAOC we would complete detailed planning, conduct a risk assessment of every aspect of the mission (bringing together aviation and maritime issues) and if acceptable I would authorise the launch from *OCEAN*. In effect we therefore had two levels of risk assessment and Go/No Go decisions – one at the CAOC and the final one by me.

On 31 May, as the reformed Task Group was heading towards Brega in eastern Libya we continued our detailed planning with the staff presenting their key conclusions. The key takeaway was the importance of real-time surveillance in prosecuting AH targets. AH are, as a battlefield helicopter, used to operating with land forces who can cue them onto targets. In more recent operations in Afghanistan this cueing was often done by unmanned aerial vehicles (UAVs) and in Libya there were simply too few UAVs available and no ground component. This was particularly frustrating since both *ALBION* and *OCEAN* were able to receive live UAV feeds – as were the CAOC – but there were simply too few UAVs in theatre and none in the RN at all, unlike the USN.

The last few days in May also saw tension between the need to meet our exercise obligations east of Suez and my focus on impending Libyan strikes. My own view was that we should retain as many units as possible for Libya but the strategic imperative remained Exercise *Sea Khanjar* on 2–8 July with the United Arab Emirates. It was therefore decided that *ALBION, SUTHERLAND* and the *BAYS* should detach on 7 June, leaving me and a reduced staff in *OCEAN* and *FORT ROSALIE* to launch AH strikes. Enabling me to command from *OCEAN* would need some preparation – not least of which would be fitting a NATO information system at sea, transferring the intelligence systems from *ALBION* and selecting which staff went east to support James Morley conducting amphibious exercises and which were key for AH operations to remain with me. This was all a week away and, to be frank, I had more pressing things to focus on.

I flew by helicopter to the French carrier *CHARLES DE GAULLE* to compare notes with Admiral Coindreau. The French had a not dissimilar organisation and approach to us. The Admiral remained in his flagship but his attack helicopter strikes would be launched from the helicopter carrier *TONNERRE*. The presence of a fixed-wing carrier did however give him more freedom of action than I had.

My AH strikes would depend on a large amount of support from the NATO air component – in terms of UAV and target surveillance and fixed-wing air support – and we were therefore firmly a small part in the larger air component effort. In theory the French had the same command and control construct as me – they were in associated support to NATO – so when their AH launched they chopped to NATO. Admiral Philippe was remarkably frank when he said that despite this, in the final resort his ships and aircraft were national assets, and he might strike when not ordered by NATO and indeed might cancel NATO-directed missions if that's what Paris ordered.

It was clear that UK and French national interests were aligned – as were our political leaders – and the French were keen to make the most of this. My reception onboard included photographs for the press with the Admiral and me in front of Union flags and *tricolores*. More importantly it meant that the Admiral and I could work without barriers – we agreed to exchange liaison officers and to keep each other fully informed of activities, particularly when in adjacent sea space. He even said that he would tell me whenever he intended to deviate for national reasons from the NATO Air Tasking Order – a promise he kept. It was a remarkably strong and effective relationship. The French were keen to strike around Brega since the front line between Gaddafi and rebel forces lay just east of the city and the French admiral felt that they had a realistic chance of encouraging the rebels to take the offensive and move west.

We continued our passage towards Libya and on 1 June we began discussing our first targets – Will Laidlaw (OC 656 Squadron) and his team, my targeter Emma Ward and Chris James in the CAOC effectively identifying potential AH targets and working them through the CAOC system until 24 hours later they came back down to us for detailed planning. Our first targets were west of Brega, a radar dome mounted 80ft above the ground and then a vehicle check point (VCP) which pro-Gaddafi forces were using to control the flow of civilians. Detailed planning consisted of the aircrew looking at aerial reconnaissance photographs of the targets and planning their attack headings, weapons, heights and routes to and from the targets.

With this all passed back to the CAOC the NATO planners and Air Commodore Ed (for the UK) would decide if the attack was suitable and the risks were acceptable, at which point the tasking would be in the Air Tasking Order (ATO), effectively giving me permission to launch the attack — subject to my own risk judgement.

One of my roles was to think the unthinkable, and armed with my knowledge of the risks I probed my team on the 'what ifs' of an AH being downed — and specifically how we could recover aircrew from hostile territory and what medical support could we provide for casualties. In both cases the answer wasn't reassuring. My Task Group did not include a surgical team and the UK had no combat search and rescue capability (CSAR) — that is helicopters and personnel, trained and equipped to pick up downed aircrew from the enemy territory. I would mitigate this risk by ensuring other NATO elements, both at sea and ashore, had the needed capabilities on specific call to assist, CSAR generally ashore in Italy and medical support afloat in NATO warships. I also asked the team to ensure that all the procedures were in place to deal with casualties and death reporting — this was serious business.

The other factor that our planning continued to highlight was the importance of messaging the Gaddafi regime in order to have the required psychological impact. The media would have an important part to play in announcing that Apaches had entered the fray. As a result we had a dozen or so journalists in the group together with a handler from the MOD's Directorate of Media Communications (DMC) supported by my own public relations officer Lieutenant Commander Jeremy Oliver. The MOD had provided very clear lines to take for the group to use with the media. They centred on describing the Apaches' ability to strike with greater accuracy that fast jets currently could, due to their capability, speed, and low height, offering a vital tool to the ongoing air operations to protect Libyan civilians. The target audience was in effect the Gaddafi regime and so I and my team began learning our lines. Doing this made me think of another issue. It was all very well me and my people appearing on TV to say how we were supporting the innocent people of Libya but at this point there appeared to be a stalemate on the ground in Libya. Gaddafi could very conceivably remain in power for months – if not longer – and was it therefore safe for our images to appear in the media? I asked the for MOD clarification and they agreed that there was indeed a potential risk to those who appeared – and as a result only those in command positions, not the actual aircrew, should appear on film. Effectively that meant myself, Andrew Betton (*OCEAN*) and Jason Etherington (CO 4 Regt) – with Apache pilots being filmed in such a way as to hide their identities.

Our preparations were complete and our first strikes appeared in the ATO. As we neared our launch position I received a number of calls – Lieutenant General Joddice (NATO Air Component Commander), General Charles Bouchard (NATO Commander), Major General Messenger (COS(Ops) at PJHQ) and finally one from Air Commodore Ed Stringer. They all had the same messages – the importance of what we were going to do, support for me and my people and seeking reassurance that I and the aircrew were content with the mission. In response I explained that we understood the psychological effect we were trying to achieve, that we appreciated the support AH were getting in terms of UAVs and fixed-wing assets, and that my priority was achieving the mission while minimising the risk to the aircrew. I also explained how all this would come together in the final Go/No Go brief onboard which would give me a final opportunity to cancel the mission if there was any significant cause for concern. The calls left me feeling extremely well supported and ready for what would follow.

On the evening of 3 June, the Task Group closed the Libyan coast. Our ships were not showing any lights and radar and communication transmissions were at a minimum. *SUTHERLAND* and *COMMANDANT BIROT* were between *OCEAN*, *ALBION* and the shore. The presence of Libyan fishing vessels and coastal radar meant that we would most likely be detected and we needed to be ready for anything. At around 2100 the key staff assembled in a semi-circle in HMS *ALBION*'s operation room and with the brief introduction from the chief of staff of, 'Ladies and gentlemen, the Commodore,' the staff came to attention and then relaxed as the Go/No Go brief commenced.

'Go/No Go brief for AH strikes against radar mast and vehicle check points in the vicinity of Brega.'

We would open with a description of the mission and the intended flight routes, heights and speeds to and from the target, what weapons would be used and a range of actions in the event of emergency or systems failure.

Then we went around the staff.

The meteorological officer would brief the weather conditions (including sea state) at launch from *OCEAN*, on the transit to and over the targets and then on the return flight. They also briefed on ambient light levels, from street lights to the moon, and how these might increase the risk of the Apaches being detected. Then based on these factors they would recommend Go or No Go.

The intelligence specialist would then brief on the expected threat from Gaddafi forces – both in terms of what Gaddafi units had been sighted in the area of the planned strikes and the weapon systems that they could be expect to deploy. They would also consider the threat to the ships of the Task Group and then give their Go/No Go recommendation.

A member of the Ops team would then brief our relative strengths. What air assets were on call to support the Apaches and how was the TG configured? Based on this did they recommend Go or No Go?

Next a staff member would brief on protection in terms of CSAR and medical. For early missions NATO CSAR was held at five hours' notice to move and we would be within an hour's flight from OCEAN to a ship carrying a surgical capability. Again, Go or No Go.

Next we would cover command and control and communications for the strike – how would the TG, Apaches, SKASAC and air component communicate with each other? Who would co-ordinate the airspace above the target – usually a NATO Airborne Early Warning and Control System (AWACS) aircraft. The detailed routing of the strike over both sea and land would be briefed. Once again, Go or No Go.

One of the staff would then cover what was happening in our adjacent sea and air space – what naval, air and specifically French activity was expected immediately before, during and after our strike and did this bring any deconfliction issues. Again based on this was it a Go or No Go recommendation.

Then David Bruce would outline the Rules of Engagement being employed – both in the air and sea and whether the strike and our supporting activity were authorised in the ATO and were compliant with the targeting directive and policy direction. He too would then recommend Go/No Go.

I then would ask the French liaison officer to comment on what the French admiral's intentions were, Jason Etherington to give a view on whether the mission was within the capabilities of the Apaches and their crews and finally James Morley as flag captain to confirm that all the units in the Task Group were in the right location and ready for the strike.

With every member of the staff recommending Go all eyes were on me and at 2200 I gave the final Go decision. Two Apaches and a supporting SKASAC would launch.

Now all I, and the staff, could do was wait. Will Laidlaw led two Apaches from *OCEAN* to the radar sight which he engaged with two Hellfire missiles, the first of 99 to be fired during the weeks ahead, and his 30mm gun – completely destroying the target. Next they flew 10km to the west to engage the vehicle check point which was now fully alerted. On arrival they detected a number of troops running around on the ground, but in themselves they presented no threat and they were not engaged. But then a technical mounting a ZU-23-2, carefully hidden under a sun shelter, opened fire on the Apaches. The ZU-23-2 is a Soviet twin 23mm autocannon which can fire between 400 and 2300 rpm (the lower figure giving more accuracy). The Apache aircrew reacted with remarkable calm – while Will Laidlaw took evading action the second helicopter fired four 20-round bursts of 30mm, destroying the technical and killing two of its crew. The survivors ran from the scene and once again in accordance with the ROE were not engaged. The stricken vehicle and its ammunition burnt wildly and the VCP was abandoned. Under 10 minutes later both Apaches were approaching *OCEAN* and safely recovered. Adjacent to us the French launched their first attack helicopter strike. The French packages tended to consist of Gazelle and Tigre helicopters, launched from FS *TONNERE*. They too returned safely having fired nine missiles at their targets.

On safely recovering the Apaches and Sea King I signalled my bosses and the MOD:

> FROM: COMUKTG
> SUBJECT/FIRST RFTG MAR STRIKE MISSION
> 1. RFTG LAUNCHED MAR STRIKE PACKAGE – 2 X AH (4 REGT AAC- 656 SQN) and I X SKASAC (857 SQN) – AT 032225ZJUN11 to ATTACK TARGETS IVO BREGA LIBYA.
> 2. MISSION COMPLETED AND ALL AIRCRAFT SAFELY RECOVERED to OCEAN 032349Z JUN 11.
> 3. RFTG READY IN ALL RESPECTS FOR FURTHER TASKING.

Then I signalled the commanding officers and therefore the men and women of the Task Group:

> FROM: COMUKTG
> SUBJECT/FIRST RFTG MAR STRIKE MISSION
> PERSONAL FROM COMMODORE
> 1. THE RFTG HAS SAFELY EXECUTED THE FIRST OPERATIONAL AH MAR STRIKE MISSION.
> 2. THIS IS A SIGNIFICANT ACHIEVEMENT FOR ALL CONCERNED. BRAVO ZULU.[3]

The next action was for the aircrew to debrief the mission including carefully scrutinising the gun tapes which graphically showed the result of Hellfire and 30mm hitting their targets. Either I or my chief of staff would watch every one of these so that if we were challenged by our own chain of command or more probably by Gaddafi's propaganda machine I would be able to account for every round we had fired and be able to refute any claims of indiscriminate killing. But it brought home to me the seriousness of the decisions I was taking – it was a responsibility I took extremely seriously. As I recorded in my journal:

Probably the most demanding evening of my service. For the first time in 27 years I order ships and aircraft into action with the very real possibility of killing the enemy and losing people.

On this first night, and for every subsequent strike, I would stay in the operations room while the helicopters were airborne, carefully monitoring their progress and willing them safely back to the ship.

The next step was to implement DMC's plan to maximise the impact of the arrival of Apaches in the media. Armed with our carefully crafted lines, we put the media plan into action. In *OCEAN*, Geraint Vincent from ITN interviewed Will Laidlaw sitting in his cockpit, but as directed carefully hiding his identity. The next day in *ALBION* Jason Etherington and I were interviewed by the collective press pack including Sky, the BBC and ITN. My first question was mischievous but predictable: 'So, Commodore, what this operation proves is that the government were wrong to dispose of the UK's aircraft carriers and Harrier force?' Thinking quickly and using my media training – respond, then bridge to the question you want to answer and then give the information you wish to pass – my reply was: 'Thank you, what I think you are asking is do we need a UK aircraft carrier for this operation. The answer is no since we are operating under the umbrella of the NATO air component proving all the air power that is needed. If you are asking does the UK need aircraft carriers for expeditionary operations in the future – the answer is yes and that is why we are building two.' Probably not the government-bashing response they wanted – and it certainly didn't make the press. The next question was, 'Commodore, what do Apaches bring to this operation that fixed-wing aircraft can't?' The DMC lines now came into play and I remembered my briefing that I was speaking directly to the Gaddafi regime. 'The unique ability of attack helicopters is due to their height, speed and sensors to identify and engage targets with huge precision that at present fixed-wing aircraft cannot. This adds an important capability to the air component and enables us to provide a level of protection to the civilian population of Libya where attack helicopters are flying which before we could not.'

Jason Etherington also stuck to his lines and was reported in the *Times* as saying, 'This is an escalation in support of the civilians who Gaddafi is persecuting. We will be given targets perhaps fast jets cannot because of the risk of collateral damage. We can fly lower and slower and have smaller, more precise weapons… The Apaches bring something else to the party.'[4] The resulting media achieved what DMC set out. The papers on 5 and 6 June contained a range of articles, the *Times* headlines being 'Out of the dark, the Apaches hit… and change the game' and 'Apache strikes aim to break the deadlock and allow rebel advance on Tripoli'. Interviews and footage of the first night's strikes were broadcast on all the major networks. The psychological effect is difficult to judge but in their book *The Cauldron* Rob Weighill and Florence Gaub wrote: 'The psychological impact was significant, due in large part to the helicopters' reputation as a lethal airborne platform that could quickly acquire and accurately engage the target. They could not be heard or seen, carried a complex array of target acquisition systems and fired lethal weapons with a high degree of precision.'[5]

★★

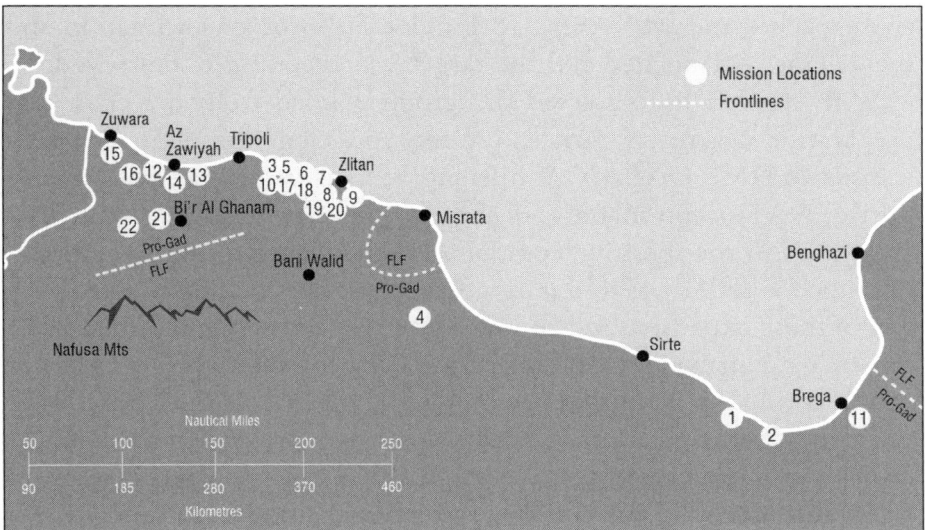

Apache Missions Flown 3 June–6 August

While the operational and tactical benefit of the strikes may have been limited there was an unexpected reaction to the strikes around Brega. During the first raid we had been monitoring the Gaddafi forces' communications and on detecting the approaching helicopters and/ or TG they stood to their defences and prepared for the amphibious assault they expected to follow. This fear of a NATO amphibious assault in the vicinity of Brega was to persist and over the weeks ahead Gaddafi forces constructed a range of beach defences in the area to counter the landings that were never planned.

With the media activity over we quickly focused on the next strike. Following the same planning and authorisation process as the first night the AH cell in the CAOC had, working with the onboard team, selected a BM-21 rocket launcher. Of Russian design, this was a truck mounting 40 122mm rockets with a range in excess of 12 miles. In many ways this was a perfect Apache target – it was carefully dug in next to a house which meant that fast jets were unable to strike it due to the risk of damaging the adjacent building. It therefore appeared as our next target in the ATO. Onboard *ALBION* the command team mustered for its second Go/No Go briefing and after receiving the recommendations of the staff it was a Go. The same size package – two Apaches and a SKASAC to provide airborne co-ordination and surveillance – launched and the target was successfully destroyed.

With the strike completed the group opened from the coast and preparation began in earnest for me and elements of my staff to transfer to HMS *OCEAN*. While engineers were hard at work setting up the NATO command and control systems in *OCEAN* an issue arose around the sensitive computers at the centre of my operational intelligence cell. I was told in no uncertain terms that there were very few of these expensive and complex systems in the UK and the risk of one being damaged while transferring between the two ships was not worth taking – if I insisted it would be at my own risk. Considering the tactical and operational insights that it was providing – helping us to both propose targets to the CAOC and keep my aircrew safe – it was a no-brainer. Thankfully it arrived and was set up in *OCEAN* without difficulty.

Selecting who on the staff went with me was also key. The balance was to provide James Morley with enough amphibious planners to conduct the east of Suez phase under his command and to give me enough to carry on with the maritime strike mission. For a short while it was suggested that a second commodore be flown out to take command of the *ALBION* group. I rejected this idea since the resulting Task Group was no bigger that that I had commanded as the captain of *ALBION*. What is more, James had proved to be an excellent flag captain and deputy commander who understood Task Group and amphibious operations – I had every confidence that he would do a first-class job. To support him he retained the majority of my staff headed by my chief of staff, Tom Guy.

OCEAN was not designed to be a flagship so space would be at a premium and unsurprisingly my picks focused largely on intelligence and aviation. Lieutenant Colonel Al Livingstone RM as SO1 ISTAR (Intelligence, Surveillance, Target Acquisition and Reconnaissance)[6] was ideally placed to head the team and became my chief of staff in *OCEAN*. On the aviation side was my SO2 Fixed Wing Aviation, Lieutenant Commander Paul Tremelling, an experienced Harrier pilot who understood the ATO and air space management. He was joined by my targeter Lieutenant Emma Ward who played such a pivotal role in helping select and develop potential targets. Since we were working with, and operating adjacent to and sometimes in the same waters as NATO submarines I also took my SO2 Submariner Lieutenant Commander Justin Hutchings who also took up the mantle as the staff operations officer. I remained concerned about the prospect of casualties and the lack of a surgical team in *OCEAN* and so my SO2 Medical Lieutenant Commander Karen Duke joined the team to provide the planning advice I needed. On the key intelligence front I had Lieutenant Wayne 'Buz' Basketfield and Warrant Officer Graeme Leslie. David Bruce was an essential member of the team and came across with us. To enable me to keep up with the administrative workload and to ensure I kept up with my own battle rhythm – being in the right place at the right time – I was accompanied by my military assistant, Lieutenant Andy Parker. I also carefully selected some of the best to be my liaison officers in other headquarters, where they could speak on my behalf and with my authority. Lieutenant Commander Steve Wren went to the NATO flagship, the Italian carrier *GARIBALDI*, and Lieutenant Commander Lyndsey Netherwood went to JHC Naples. In return I welcomed Lieutenant Colonel Bernard Vettori from the French admiral's staff to my team.

Transferring to *OCEAN* had a number of advantages – none more than the fact it brought my planners and me together with the aircrews planning and conducting the missions. I could therefore slim down the aviation staff structure. Jason Etherington remained as both my SO1 AH and my Joint Helicopter Commands representative – known as the Operational Duty Holders Representative. In this role he had a responsibility to inform me if anything we planned for the AH was outside the aircraft or crews' capabilities. It was a relationship that could not have worked better. Jason gave me excellent advice and support throughout and we were as one in sharing the priority of mitigating the risk – as far as we could – to our aircrew. From HMS *OCEAN* I could rely on the excellent Commander (Air) – known as Wings – Lieutenant Colonel Lenny Brown RM, an experienced helicopter pilot who would both deliver the flying programme and keep on top of aviation standards for the variety of aircraft operating from his deck. His captain, Andrew Betton, would prove to be a similarly good flag captain, looking after the flagship and getting the remaining ships of the group in the right place at the right time and co-ordinating with those under NATO command. In terms of the daily interface between the staff and the ship there were three key *OCEAN* players who really made it work – from the operations team Lieutenant Commanders Ben Keith and Simon Collins, and Lenny's deputy, or 'little wings', Lieutenant Commander Jim Corbett.

We were planning to cross deck on Tuesday 7 June, with all the systems in *OCEAN* being set to work in preparation for our arrival on the 6th. Operationally we were repositioning and preparing to strike targets in between Zlitan and Tripoli, some 300nm west of Brega. Unlike Brega this would be a far more testing proposition since the majority of Gaddafi's best equipped and trained units were in this area.

As I grappled with changing flagship, bedding down a new streamlined staff and preparing for more demanding operations I was hit by a bombshell. Back in the UK CJO had been briefed by an RAF officer that the media coverage we had generated was not aimed at Gaddafi but at undermining fast jets and therefore by association the Royal Air Force. This was clearly a continuation of the bad feeling between the RN and RAF that I had seen in the MOD and the result was an order from PJHQ ordering me to hand over all my command responsibilities to the CO *OCEAN* and depart the Mediterranean. I had been sacked. I was dumbstruck, confused and, to be honest, angry — my team and I were working under immense pressure to deliver an untried capability in testing circumstances and had been meticulous in not deviating from the DMC lines, all approved by the MOD.

I kept my sacking to myself and the next day spoke to Major General Gordon Messenger in Northwood to find out exactly what was going on. I explained that we had DMC handlers with us and that we had all used the approved lines — the target audience was not the UK defence community but Gaddafi. General Gordon was as good, and pragmatic, as ever — he knew CJO had been incorrectly briefed but it would not be easy to get a quick reversal of the decision. To help I should carry on delivering at the sharp end and produce a plan that while moving to transfer command to Andrew would effectively highlight why it simply wasn't a sensible option. All media from *OCEAN* was to cease. It was the sensible way to address the issue but it left me feeling very uncomfortable and uncertain about my future — but thankfully I had enough to focus on to distract me from the issue.

The move west was a significant one. In early June there was a sense that the campaign had stalled. Rebels held Benghazi in the west with a front line with pro-Gaddafi forces (PGF) to the east of Brega. The other significant rebel stronghold remained the port city of Misrata — which had been the focus of our early planning on the deployment. Immediately west of Misrata was Zlitan where Gaddafi's 32 Brigade, commanded by his son Khamis, was located. Not only was Khamis an effective career soldier, 32 Bde was a 10,000-strong force equipped with the full range of tanks, armoured vehicles, artillery and rocket launchers. More worryingly for us it had countless anti-aircraft weapons including the latest SA-24 MANPADS. 32 Bde's capability was complemented by Gaddafi's Special Forces who were based just 20nm west of the brigade around Al Khums. Determined and well-equipped fighters, they brought the additional complication of fast boats and inflatables able to operate along the Libyan coast and behind rebel lines. Khamis' 32 Bde had effectively been given the task of destroying the rebels' enclave within Misrata and NATO HQ expected a major co-ordinated offensive against the city soon.

Having transferred to *OCEAN* I detached *ALBION, SUTHERLAND* and the *BAYS* to head east for their Middle East programme. *ALBION* and *SUTHERLAND* steamed past the new flagship exchanging salutes as they went – normally paid by bosun's call, Roger Readwin going so far as to fire an 11-gun salute – that paid to a commodore. Not required nor requested, it certainly showed style. I also phoned Commodore Tim Fraser who was the UK Maritime Component Commander in the Gulf to effectively hand over the *ALBION* group to his care. Although I had certain administrative responsibilities for them he would be their operational tasker and I wanted to brief him on the rather ad hoc group he was receiving – and also to reassure him that in James Morley he had a very capable commander and supporting staff.

As the team began exploring and developing potential targets in the vicinity of Zlitan I got to work on the note outlining the risks of handing over command to Andrew. At the heart of the direction was the misunderstanding of how a Task Group works and that *OCEAN* was simply an airfield like any ashore, providing aircraft to service an ATO. Andrew as the flag captain had a key role. Not only was he my deputy but also he had to ensure that the ships and aircraft were in the right place both to deliver strikes and to protect *OCEAN*. This meant co-ordinating at the tactical level with RN ships and NATO platforms. My role was really two-fold – the up-and-out with the myriad of organisations and commands and also the risk management judgement for the strikes. I sent in the paper and my continued presence was immediately supported by Admiral Corder ... but we would have to wait to see.

The next strike was scheduled for 9 June. The target was a command and control centre on the coast to the west of Tripoli within 32 Brigade's area. The very real prospect of MANPADs on the coast to defend the centre meant that the Apache crews selected a route that would take them overland away from the target and enable them to attack from an unexpected direction. The Go/No Go brief highlighted the much-increased threat levels and indeed the array of anti-aircraft systems that the Apaches might encounter. I relied on the CAOC's and Apache crews' assessment of the threat — the CAOC had already given a Go and the threat briefers and Jason Etherington recommended a Go at my decision brief but I resolved to ask PJHQ to address the shortfall in our onboard medical facilities and the lack of a dedicated combat search and rescue capability. This would be work for the day ahead and based on the briefing and the recommendations from all the team I gave the Go decision.

The Apaches launched just before midnight and despite not taking the direct route they found the Gaddafi troops waiting for them. As they crossed the coast they were immediately engaged by a shoulder-launched SA-24 fired from the sand dunes. The SA-24 is the latest variant of Russian MANPAD, entering service in 2004. Equipped with an infra-red homing system, it has a maximum engagement height of 20,000ft and approaches the target at over Mach 2. It is rightly regarded as one of the most effective helicopter killers in the world — and one was in flight towards the Apaches. Thankfully the Apaches' automated warning and defensive aids systems came to life, alerting the aircrew and firing a series of flares to decoy the missile. The Apache had won and the missile exploded — but it had got uncomfortably close, one of the pilots reporting that it was close enough to see the missile's shape and markings. The aircrews' training now kicked in and the Apaches' weapons systems and sensors were slewed to the SA-24 firing position where the infra-red camera picked up the firer appearing to go for a second launcher. The result was awfully predictable and a burst of 30mm gunfire effectively removed the threat. While one Apache was dealing with the SA-24 the other put two Hellfire missiles into the C2 node and then both returned safely to *OCEAN*.

The next day was business as usual – for a non-strike day. The round of meetings, briefings and calls went on. Paul Abraham phoned me (it was usually the other way round) and I also talked to Admirals Corder and Potts; all were pleased with the way the Task Group was performing so far. That afternoon I said goodbye to COMMANDANT BIROT. The French frigate had stayed with me after ALBION and SUTHERLAND had detached but its time with the Task Group was now up and it was required to return to national tasking off the French coast. The captain, Commander Thibault de Possesse, had played a full part in the Group and enjoyed my complete confidence. He made no secret of how much he and his ship had enjoyed being part of the Group and his disappointment at having to depart for what he regarded as less important tasking. An officer with real potential and talent; I was sorry to see him and his fine ship depart.

On the Apache side the Zlintan raid had amply demonstrated the risks involved with flying AH against Gaddafi formations and I lobbied hard for an organic combat search and rescue capability and for a medical surgical team to be embarked in OCEAN. Such was the support I was receiving from Ian Corder and his HQ that a novel solution to the CSAR gap was found: a dedicated US CSAR unit based in Italy would join and operate from OCEAN, significantly reducing the flight time to recover downed aircrew. At the same time Karen Duke was developing plans to get a surgical team to the ship.

At this point my intelligence cell really paid dividends by identifying a maritime Apache target. NATO submarines and air surveillance had recognised a pattern of small boat activity from the Al Khums-based Gaddafi SF. Every night two small rigid-hull inflatable boats (RHIBs) were detected transiting the coast and re-supplying Gaddafi artillery positions around Misrata. Over the previous few nights they had been observed close inshore by the submarine TRIUMPH and then by its relief on station, the French submarine AMETHYSTE. This seemed to me to be a good maritime target. Not only would it prevent munitions reaching Gaddafi forces, it would also strike at his SF capability – and in recent weeks we had seen these RHIBs laying mines in the approaches to Misrata. The Apaches would be feet wet

HMS *ARGYLL* (2nd command). (Author's collection)

HMS *PURSUER* (1st command). (Author's collection)

HMS *PURSUER* (1st command). (Author's collection)

HMS *ALBION* sails from Devonport, 7 April 2011. (Royal Navy Archive, Open Government Licence)

The integrated COMUKTG/3 Cdo Bde Staff. (Author's collection)

The command team (from left): Colonel Hayden White, Commander Landing Force; the author, COMUKTG; Captain James Morley, Flag Captain (HMS *ALBION*). (Author's collection)

HMS *SUTHERLAND*. (Author's collection)

Commander Roger Readwin (HMS *SUTHERLAND*) and COMUKTG. (Author's collection)

Exercise *Cypriot Wader*, RFA *MOUNTS* and *CARDIGAN BAY*. (Royal Navy Archive, Open Government Licence)

HMS *OCEAN* and *WAVE KNIGHT* replenish, as seen from *ALBION*. (Author's collection)

Flagship HMS *ALBION* during *Cypriot Lion* wearing COMUKTG's broad pennant. (Author's collection)

HMS *ALBION* docked down during *Cypriot Lion*. (Author's collection)

Battle staff onboard HMS *ALBION* (from left): COMUKTG; Commander Richard Harris (SO1 Logistics); Lieutenant Commander Tim Neald (Staff Operations Officer); Lieutenant Colonel Al Livingstone (SO1 ISTAR). (Author's collection)

HMS *ALBION* in Souda Bay, 3 May 2011. (Author's collection)

HMS *OCEAN* joins the Task Group, Souda Bay, 8 May 2011. (Author's collection)

FNS *COMMANDANT BIROT.* (Author's collection)

COMUKTG and Commander Thibault de Possesse (*BIROT*). (Author's collection)

HMS *ALBION* replenishes from *FORT ROSALIE*. (Author's collection)

RFA *FORT ROSALIE*. (Author's collection)

Maritime strike: HMS *OCEAN* with Apache and USAF HH-60 on deck. (Royal Navy Archive, Open Government Licence)

The COMUKTG staff transferred to *OCEAN*: COMUKTG flanked by Lieutenant Colonel Jason Etherington (SO1 AH) and Lieutenant Colonel Al Livingstone (now Chief of Staff). (Author's collection)

Apache. (Author's collection)

16 July USAF HH60 with SKASAC in background. (Royal Navy Archive, Open Government Licence)

The 4 June interview with the press that resulted in the author being ordered out of the Mediterranean. (Author's collection)

Lieutenant Colonel Jason Etherington briefing COMUKTG on the Apache. (Royal Navy Archive)

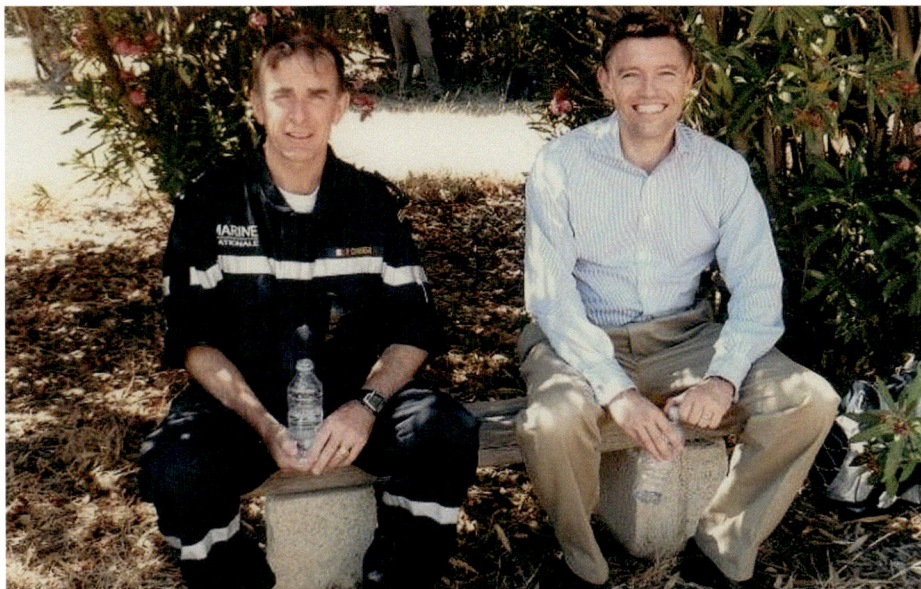

Brothers in arms Rear Admiral Philippe Coindreau and COMUKTG waiting for a flight to Naples in Malta, 9 July 2011. (Author's collection)

RFAs *ORANGELEAF, FORT ROSALIE* and *HMS SUTHERLAND* replenish, 31 July 2011. (Author's collection)

HMS *LIVERPOOL*. (Royal Navy Archive, Open Government Licence)

HMS *BANGOR* alongside HMS *OCEAN*. (Author's collection)

Flagship HMS *OCEAN* alongside in Malta. (Author's collection)

HMS *OCEAN* command team (from left): Commander Paul Pitcher (HMS *OCEAN* Executive Officer); Captain Andrew Betton (Flag Captain and HMS *OCEAN*); COMUKTG; Lieutenant Andrew Parker (Military Assistant to COMUKTG). (Author's collection)

The author onboard HMS *OCEAN*. (Author's collection)

RFA *FORT ROSALIE*. (Author's collection)

HMS *LIVERPOOL* returns to Portsmouth. (Royal Navy Archive, Open Government Licence)

throughout and therefore at reduced missile threat. The Apache cell and Emma Ward proposed to the CAOC that we place Apaches on deck alert and wait for the RHIBs to be located, and then use a SKASAC to vector them onto the boats for a strike. As long as the SKASAC could track them and establish their point of origin they would be a legitimate target. Unlike overland missions the aircraft would not chop to NATO and would remain under my command – all we required was a flying slot in the ATO. I also asked the legal team what our responsibilities would be for recovering any survivors in the water from the strike. As with recovering our own aircrew there was very little I could actually do, since none of my helicopters could winch at night. But survivors are survivors and I wanted to know if I was obliged to send my own small boats into Libyan territorial waters to recover them. I was surprised when the legal advice came back to say that because they were so close inshore their rescue was the responsibility of the Gaddafi regime. I was both relieved that my people would not be put at greater risk by a rescue attempt but deeply saddened by the prospects for anyone left in the water.

The 12 June was developing into a potentially busy night. Not only were we on call for the potential RHIB strike but the CAOC had allocated a Predator UAV to search for targets in the vicinity of a pro-Gaddafi VCP on the Zlitan-Misrata road. The plan was to keep the Apaches at deck alert and launch them when the SKASAC had located the RHIBs before returning to *OCEAN* to await potential tasking from the Predator. The Go/No Go brief was conducted as usual and two Apaches were placed on deck alert and a SKASAC launched. Developed from the original Sea King Airborne Early Warning whose Searchwater radar combined with air traffic control capability provided protection for the fleet, 857 RNAS Sea King ASAC was a much more capable beast. With an enhanced mission system, comms and data links it could provide force protection but also high quality surveillance over both land and sea. It was ideal for cueing maritime strikes and tonight was no different.

The Gaddafi RHIBs had simply become too predictable. Within minutes of placing the Apaches on deck alert the SKASAC was tracking them along their normal route towards the *AMETHYSTE*. The Apaches launched, checked in with the air co-ordinator and were chopped to the SKASAC's radio frequency who vectored them to the targets. The gun tapes from this engagement – and I studied virtually all of them – were revealing. Firstly, the aircrew could make out the periscopes of *AMETHYSTE* as it continued its demanding surveillance operation. Then the remarkable skill of the Apache crews to hit fast-moving boats with their 30mm guns – and of course the awful consequence as both boats were hit. Less than 10 minutes later both helicopters were back on *OCEAN*'s deck.

It would be a very short pause. As they were landing we were receiving reports that the Predator had detected a ZSU-23-4 hidden in a copse near one of the VCPs. With a suck of fuel both Apaches launched once again into the dark Mediterranean night and NATO command. Time was valuable since the Predator was nearing the end of its mission with about 15 minutes of fuel left before it had to go off task. The complexity of modern warfare is perhaps best demonstrated by an Apache pilot over Libya being vectored onto a target by a Predator whose pilot was sitting in the US Creech Air Force base near Las Vegas. The Predator used its laser to identify the target to the Apaches and a moment later the ZSU was destroyed by a Hellfire missile. Following the missile strike the area around the VCP came alive with pro-Gaddafi forces – the front line blockading Misrata. Both Apaches engaged the VCP and with their work done they headed north back to the sea and HMS *OCEAN*.

Ambient lighting was a major factor when planning strike operations and a feature of the lunar cycle is that for about a week a month the moon is at its brightest – during which low-flying helicopters become vulnerable to detection. This was not a good week to fly strikes but did provide a useful tempo for *OCEAN* to go off task and for everyone to rest and recuperate. Monday 13 June therefore saw *OCEAN* heading towards Augusta in Sicily. The normal round of meetings carried on – but the previous evening's strikes made very positive news at the Fleet Command Group. Still no news on reversing my removal so I simply got on with the job.

We arrived alongside the following day and I was pleased to welcome onboard the attack helicopter team from Naples (including Jack Davis and Chris James) and Air Commodore Stringer's replacement, and the new senior Brit at the CAOC, Air Commodore Gary Waterfall. The key role of this cell in developing AH targets with those afloat and then getting them through the CAOC's processes was working extremely well — thanks in no small part to the real understanding between those in the cell and in *OCEAN*. Another day saw another note from me to Fleet HQ explaining why I needed to remain in *OCEAN*.

Our return to sea on 16 June saw the arrival of three HH-60G Pave Hawk helicopters and combat search and rescue teams from the US Air Force's 56th Rescue Squadron. This was an important step, effectively filling the gap in the UK's CSAR capability and meaning that we no longer would depend upon helicopters launched from Italy. It was also a challenge for HMS *OCEAN* and particularly Wings, Lieutenant Colonel Lenny Brown. Lenny was overseeing a unique air group — UK Army Apaches, RN SKASAC and Lynx and now USAF Pave Hawks. While the ship would integrate the various personnel, Lenny had to ensure that all the aircrew were safe to operate from *OCEAN*'s deck. He and his team devised and oversaw a flying programme to achieve this before our next planned strikes. The men and women of the 56th quickly settled into the ship and you could not fail to be impressed by their can-do attitude and professionalism. Importantly I knew the Apaches' crews joined me in feeling reassured that we now had a good chance of recovering any aircrew downed in Libya.

Saturday 18 June was the next strike day. In the morning I flew by Lynx to visit the destroyer HMS *LIVERPOOL* within Libyan territorial waters. *LIVERPOOL* had already had an eventful deployment and was playing an important part in both enforcing the arms blockade on Gaddafi and supporting the civilian population in Misrata. In April the boarding team had detected an illegal cargo in a merchant ship that was subsequently diverted away from Libya and on 12 May the ship had returned fire on a Gaddafi rocket artillery site that had engaged it. Its duties often took it into Libyan territorial waters as it provided important surveillance of the coast, ensured the port of Misrata remained open and stood by to provide assistance to the civilian population. In addition, *LIVERPOOL's* aircraft controllers were providing direction for NATO aircraft and the ship would be used to provide protection for the *OCEAN* group as we closed the coast to conduct strikes.

LIVERPOOL was undoubtedly a well-led and -run ship – the positive and upbeat atmosphere I had experienced during my visit in Portsmouth was still very much in evidence, now with an added operational focus. Hosted by the commanding officer, Commander Colin Williams, and his excellent XO, Lieutenant Commander Andrew Canale, I greatly valued meeting Colin's people and also discussing with him how the campaign might develop. One of the NATO Task Group's roles was preventing small fast pro-Gaddafi boats from resupplying Gaddafi forces around Misrata and also laying mines in the approaches to the harbour. Our Apaches had proved that they were a very capable way of interdicting this traffic and I felt that sort of tasking should be considered by the NATO Task Group Commander – Apaches working with the on-station NATO destroyers and frigates could provide an impressive capability. I decided that this was one to raise with Rear Admiral Foffi.

Colin was rightly concerned that his people should get the recognition they deserved and felt that the Royal Navy's (and *LIVEROOOL's*) efforts were not getting the attention they merited. I agreed with him, but was able to give the context of why there was real sensitivity about any naval stories coming out of the Libyan campaign – without revealing the personal difficulties that I was facing as a result of those first media interviews. My advice to Colin was as much to myself: all we could do was concentrate on the mission and whatever the outcome the Royal Navy would know what the ships and men and women of the Task Group had done. I also briefed Colin on the strike missions that *OCEAN* was conducting and explained that the departure of *COMMANDANT BIROT* and *SUTHERLAND* meant that I would increasingly look to *LIVERPOOL* to provide protection for *OCEAN*.

The visit confirmed my high opinion of *LIVERPOOL* but made me ask some questions about the different approaches of the UK battle staff and the NATO team in the Italian aircraft carrier *GARIBALDI*. My team in *OCEAN* were looking for ways of utilising Apaches in the maritime strike role and on 12 June had proved that Apaches could be a valuable weapon against small fast boats that we knew pro-Gaddafi SF were using to threaten Misrata. I would need to get Rear Admiral Foffi to think along the same lines. In addition, the UK staff had a thorough understanding of the air campaign to which we were contributing and especially the targeting directive and ATO. The directive had important read across to ships since it laid down no-fire areas and the types of munitions that could be used against particular targets – including on the coast. I did not get the same sense from the NATO Task Group which seemed to be focused on scheduling the arrival and departure of ships from coastal patrols and the interdiction of potential embargo breakers rather than the criteria for striking targets ashore. As a result, I had a growing sense that *LIVERPOOL* might not be getting the top cover (support and guidance) it needed – particularly when using its 4.5in gun. I made a note to myself to ensure my warfare team kept, whenever they could, a helpful eye on *LIVERPOOL*.

That evening's strike was a pro-Gaddafi command and control node in the vicinity of Misrata. On arriving overhead the target the Apache crews could not detect any obvious target – they could see unarmed people moving around tents but keeping to their Rules of Engagement they showed the required (and commendable) restraint and did not engage. Both Apaches turned for home but as they approached the coast they were engaged by another deadly SA-24 guided missile. This time the missile was seen by the crew before the helicopters' automated systems came to life and fired the full range of flares – that at the very last moment decoyed the incoming missile. The Apaches quickly located the SA-24 firing position – the infra-red camera revealing a multi-barrelled launcher on a flat-back truck with a still warm barrel pointing into the air and its crew fleeing from the scene. Within seconds a Hellfire was sent on its way and destroyed the truck and its launcher.

In *OCEAN* I shared the aircrews' relief at surviving a second SA-24 missile but felt it was only a matter of time before our luck ran out, and asked if there was anything more we could do to minimise the risks. The first thing we did was send all the information from the MANPAD attacks to the Air Warfare centre at RAF Waddington in Lincolnshire. Part of the RAF's Air Command, the Centre rapidly analysed the data, put this together with the known parameters of SA-24 and within 48 hours were able to provide guidance on how to best minimise the effectiveness of the missile. Armed with this advice I asked Jason Etherington to set about producing a Lessons Identified paper which, when complete, I would forward to Gary Waterfall.

The risk/reward balance was a fine one and I remained of the view that it was very likely that we would lose an aircraft at some stage – the question for the CAOC and ultimately CJO and London was whether such a loss would be acceptable. In the meantime, I would continue to try, with the CAOC, to minimise the risk as best I could. The strike for 19 June was cancelled due to there being no actionable target – the targets were out there but without surveillance and cueing Apaches could not be vectored into the right place and we were not going to launch them against the Gaddafi defences blind. Significantly, 19 June also saw Gaddafi announce a financial reward for any NATO aircraft shot down – and attack helicopters were the most vulnerable. At the forefront of my mind was the potential psychological impact on the entire campaign of losing an Apache. Two days after the introduction of the NATO aircraft bounty the United States Navy lost a Fire Scout remotely piloted helicopter drone near Zlitan. Predictably, Libyan state TV showed images of downed helicopter parts and pro-Gaddafi forces celebrating shooting down an Apache. As I suspected the regime would maximise the effect of getting an Apache – if they could.

OCEAN subsequently headed back to the east – we were returning to support the French effort around Brega. The break in strike missions enabled me to focus on paperwork. Jason Etherington's Lessons Identified note was sent and well received by Gary Waterfall – above all else it highlighted the vulnerabilities and strengths of Apaches and the need for persistent ISTAR (UAVs) to both identify targets and provide the situational awareness needed to give warning of Gaddafi air defences. The issue of my removal rumbled on. At the Fleet

Command Group the Deputy Commander in Chief, Vice Admiral George Zambellas, could not have been more supportive of my role and later in the week Paul Abraham told me that, as I suspected, I was a victim of the poisonous atmosphere in the MOD that continued between some elements of the RN and RAF. Rear Admiral Corder had, Paul said, gone in hard in support but there had been no movement on the decision to remove me – either way. What did happen was that an article that had been prepared for *Jane's Defence Weekly* on the Task Group's activities had – despite being initially cleared by the relevant PJHQ lead – been stopped. It was clear that no further news stories from *OCEAN* would get out. The uncertainty of my position was draining but I decided to simply focus on the task – and to be frank I continued to have enough to be getting on with.

During the passage we met up with the ever-dependable *FORT ROSALIE*. The replenishment ship was in a logistics routine by which we met up every two weeks to resupply *OCEAN* and its aircraft with vital stores. It played a crucial role in enabling us to remain on station and on this occasion transferred an additional Apache to us – bringing the number to five onboard.

The French focus had remained on the eastern front around Brega where they felt that a rebel breakthrough remained on the cards. They believed that combined fast jet and co-ordinated UK and French AH strikes might make the difference. The French had set up a Helicopter Planning Group in the helicopter carrier *TONNERRE* and while I kept in close touch with Admiral Coindreau we took the opportunity to send our own Apache planning team to *TONNERRE* – both to get an update on the situation around Brega and perhaps more importantly to share their experiences of AH strikes. Gaddafi had, since our first strike on 3 June, strengthened his Brega forces – including with a battalion from the elite 32 Brigade which we had encountered around Zlitan. So we could expect greater opposition than before and the French had been flying in and around Brega since then, meaning there would be no element of surprise. I was well aware of the tremendous bravery the Apache aircrews were showing launching against the latest generation MANPADs night after night but at least they benefited from the impressive self-defence systems in the Apache. Their French counterparts did not and although the Tigre is a capable attack helicopter the majority of the French formation were Gazelles – an old aircraft with very basic strike and defence capabilities. Indeed, their defence depended largely on flying in formation – four Gazelles in line abreast with a Tigre on each wing – some protection but a group of helicopters to fire at rather than a pair in loose formation. We all had huge respect for the French aircrew.

The plan for Friday 24 June was the most complex yet. Fast jets would strike a command and control node west of Brega and a radio mast to the south. Immediately after this French and UK attack helicopters would simultaneously strike in adjacent areas around the city. The French would strike to the east of the city. We would strike two groups of targets – one south of the city including a vehicle check point (VCP) near an industrial centre and wood, and then Brega airport, the second group in and around Misrata harbour. For the first time therefore, we would launch two pairs of Apaches. There would be ample ISTAR and fixed-wing support and this would be an opportunity to demonstrate what well co-ordinated and supported AH strikes might achieve. Such was the complexity of what was being planned that the onboard team – and the AH cell in the CAOC – worked flat out to prepare the mission and get us to the evening's Go/No Go decision brief. The recent SA-24 engagements and the very apparent risk focused the minds of all at these briefs – and made me acutely aware of the potential implications of the decision I gave. The CAOC had already authorised the mission but this was the last opportunity for any of the team to voice concerns and effectively stop the launch. Jason Etherington had a key role speaking on behalf of the aircrew and since the first strikes the pilots themselves would attend the Go/No Go briefs, standing just outside the circle of officers briefing but taking in every word. When I gave the Go decisions I was always aware of them looking intently at me and I took every decision to launch extremely seriously.

As we approached the planned launch time *OCEAN* turned north into the wind to generate the wind over deck to launch the first two

Apaches... but some minor aircraft defects resulted in a 20-minute delay in the entire mission. The launch took place and they were soon on their way, but for whatever reason the mission delay message was not received or acted upon in *TONNERRE* and the French AH launched at the original time, beginning their strikes before the fast jets and Apaches. Any element of surprise was lost. The pair of Apaches striking south of Brega had to be well inland to be in the right strike position after the fast jets had done their part. The jets struck as planned and immediately afterwards the Apaches' infra-red cameras detected a technical preparing to engage them — and quickly destroyed it with a Hellfire. This brought a number of Gaddafi nearby positions to life and an anti-aircraft gun immediately opened fire on the helicopters and was silenced by 30mm gun. With the anti-aircraft gun silenced the Apaches' defensive systems detected an incoming SA-6 missile. Normally launched from a vehicle, the SA6 is initially guided to its target from the ground via a command link but has a semi-active radar homing head. Flying over Mach 2 and with a range of 15 miles it is a deadly threat. The Apaches fired flares and went low — very low — to evade the missile and succeeded. The pair turned towards the airfield where a vehicle on the runway was destroyed before they turned north towards the sea and HMS *OCEAN*.

The second pair of Apaches had, since they were striking the harbour, less far to fly to their targets and launched some 15 minutes after the first two. This meant that as they approached the coast the French attack was well underway and the Gaddafi forces were on full alert; tracer was streaking into the sky around the city and where the other Apaches were in action. The coastal strike was supported by a Predator UAV — which was inexplicably unable to locate any targets in an area where intelligence suggested there were plenty. The Apaches decided to use their own systems (and the infra-red camera) to find the targets themselves and as they approached the coast they too were engaged by a missile — this time a MANPAD. This one was far too close for comfort but again the flares and the pilots' skills enabled them to evade the threat. As was now becoming the norm the launching position was then quickly engaged by Hellfire. The Apaches kept searching the ground with their cameras and then detected a MANPAD team preparing to fire at them – and they too were taken out by a Hellfire. The two helicopters then took turns (one cueing the other) to hit defended positions and vehicles in and around Brega harbour. With their ammunition expended they too turned north towards the sea and OCEAN.

As for every strike I was in or near the operations room and as the four Apaches turned for home I quickly became aware of a major – indeed life-threatening – problem. The Apaches had launched with a pre-planned position to return to on completion of the strike where they would find OCEAN. It was OCEAN's job to ensure that it was in the right place at the right time. Unfortunately, the delay in launching had opened the range from the coast and taken the ship away from its planned position, with the result that as the Apaches opened from the coast the ship was 20nm further north than it was supposed to be. The ship's team had missed this and the question was not only whether the Apaches would find us but also if they had enough fuel to reach OCEAN. The first pair arrived at the original recovery position to find no OCEAN but did manage to gain radio contact and were vectored towards the ship – it was some 20nm away and they had fuel for approximately 30nm of flying. It was going to be very tight. On sighting the ship they had enough fuel for a single approach and thankfully safely recovered. The second pair had slightly more fuel remaining and were also recovered safely. In the operations room there was no need for me to say anything – OCEAN's team knew that a basic mistake had come close to losing aircraft and crews. Andrew Betton made his people aware that this was not good enough and went to find the aircrew to apologise – the mark of the man. I too found Will Laidlaw who had led the first two aircraft and made him aware that I knew how close we had come to disaster and that I was confident that OCEAN would not let anything like it happen again.

CHAPTER SIX

Maritime Strike – Towards Success

I was by now in a well-established routine. My world revolved around my small cabin/office located right aft in the ship, the staff planning room in which Al Livingstone would co-ordinate the staff effort and the ship's operations room in which the Go/No Go briefings were held and where I would wait for the return of the helicopters from each mission. The battle rhythm that had worked so well in *ALBION* worked in *OCEAN*. My day would generally start around 0900 – noting that on strike nights we would have been up for most of the night – with a morning update brief in the operations room. This would generally be followed by catch-ups with Al Livingstone (Chief of Staff), Jason Etherington (SO 1AH) and Andrew Betton (Flag Captain). The day would revolve around staff work and Al Livingstone would prove to be an excellent COS – his response to my regular comment that 'I think we need a paper on this' was to quickly produce a draft that captured all the key points and needed little additional work. In and around this I had the round of various video conferences with the UK and the phone calls that needed to be made each week. On Monday morning I attended the Fleet Command Group by video conference. Chaired by either the Commander in Chief (Admiral Sir Trevor Soar) or Deputy Commander in Chief (Vice Admiral George Zambellas), this focused on Fleet activity and enabled me to both update on our progress, raise any issues and ask for any support we needed. On Thursdays there was a similar video conference meeting called the Operations Group chaired by Rear Admiral Ian Corder – my direct boss who in turn reported to both CINCFFLEET and CJO. Throughout the operation I was surprised by how little long-handled screwdriving took place – I was left very much on my own to make key decisions and judgements. I did, however, keep the initiative by keeping all concerned informed of what was going on and firing in a range of papers with ideas and recommendations to assist longer term planning and sustain the force. Then there were the phone calls. In an average week I would speak to Admirals Potts (UKMARFOR), Corder (COMOPS), Harding (NATO Deputy Joint Commander), Westbrook (NATO Deputy Maritime Commander), Coindreau (French TG) and Air Commodore Stringer (CAOC). I spoke virtually every day to Captain Abraham in Northwood. There were signals and intelligence reports to be read and UK ships in the NATO groups to be supported. In the evening there would be an evening command brief – followed by 'secrets' when the COS, flag captain and I would be briefed on the most sensitive intelligence. After this the flag captain and COS would draft the nightly intentions signal for the Task Group to get the ships in the right place for the following day's activities. Finally, on a strike night it would be into the Go/ No Go decision brief and then the strike itself. Throughout, a useful source of intelligence was Sky News that was nearly constantly on in my cabin and staff planning room. In terms of relaxation, I would try to get enough sleep, read a little and get a run in on the flight deck whenever flying operations allowed.

The 25 June was a strike day that followed the usual pattern. That strike was planned against a vehicle check point in the vicinity of Ra's Lanuf just to the west of Brega. That evening's Go/No Go brief did not, however, go smoothly. As usual we began with the 'Met Man's meteorological/environment input – given tonight by a new briefer. The young and slightly nervous lieutenant in effect said it was touch and go over the ship, over the target and on the helicopters' return. I thanked him and asked whether he was recommending a Go or No Go decision. He repeated the same brief and again made no recommendation. I stopped the brief and said we would start again in 30 minutes when he had sufficient information to make a recommendation. I asked the Chief of Staff and Flag Captain to make sure he got the message that he shouldn't worry about giving a recommendation that he thought I didn't want to hear – if he recommended No Go we wouldn't fly and in either case the decision rested with me. At the second brief a rather more confident brief saw him recommend Go. The strike launched as planned and destroyed three pro-Gaddafi technicals in the vicinity of the checkpoint before safely returning to the ship.

On Monday 27 June I visited Admiral Foffi in his flagship, the aircraft carrier *GARIBALDI*. He was a charming host and we shared our experiences thus far. My aim was to ensure that *LIVERPOOL* – part of the Admiral's Task Group – was getting the support it needed in terms of understanding the wider NATO maritime and more importantly air campaign with regards to no-fire areas and the required precision needed against certain targets. In addition, I wanted to encourage him to consider using AH against the Gaddafi SF small boats that were continuing to operate. The Admiral made the right noises and said his staff would work on both issues – but it was apparent that they had not been high on his priorities. He was much more comfortable scheduling ships in and out of the coastal area on surveillance and cargo interception tasking. It was nonetheless a good visit and I left feeling that I had got my messages across – time would tell.

Back in *OCEAN* the focus was on providing further advice on the risk/reward balance of AH operations – and ensuring that all concerned realised the significant risk that the Apache crews were undertaking and appreciated the psychological impact the strikes were undoubtedly having on the Gaddafi forces. This led to some interesting conversations with Gary Waterfall on who owned what risk and the status of the Go/ No Go briefs that we both held. Gary was a good colleague to work with – an experienced Harrier pilot who had operated from ships and had a good sense of the maritime domain. But there was always a slight tension between the shore-based fast jet approach where an operating base simply provides jets for tasking, and operating helicopters from the sea which requires a much closer integration between the ship and aircraft. The relationship worked since we both had the same objectives – to as far as possible reduce the risk to the aircrew. The CAOC's Go decision effectively authorised the mission in terms of supporting airpower, air command and control and targeting/ROE; my decision took these as read but added the local conditions (including sea state and maritime threat) and latest intelligence picture before launch. Critically it included confirmation from Jason Etherington as Joint Helicopter Command's representative that the tasking was within the aircraft and crews' capabilities and provided direct input from the crews themselves. Both decision processes were therefore entirely complementary in nature – in short, together they provided the required oversight and worked well.

It was also good to have an officer of the same rank outside my command chain to share issues and concerns with. I was very aware that while I was dealing with my fair share of politics (with a small p) Gary was, as a national red card holder, in a sometimes difficult position within a coalition headquarters. For me it was slightly simpler – I was firmly under UK command, liaising as needed with NATO; Gary was dealing daily with all the complexity of the national/NATO command.

For the time being my note on risk/reward was shared in draft form with my one-up (COMOPS) and Gary. Helpfully it provided my lines to take at a video call on 30 June with Joint Helicopter Command (JHC) at which Commander Land Forces (General Nick Parker) was reassured that AH were being allocated critical targets and both he and Commander JHC (Air Vice Marshall Andy Dixon) got a sense of the various measures that were in place at the CAOC and afloat to minimise the risk to aircrew.

★★

Friday 1 July was our next strike night. The front line around Brega had remained largely static and so we headed further west than ever before – our next hunting ground would be west of Tripoli. The aim was to be less predictable and utilise *OCEAN's* ability to manoeuvre over 400nm in 24 hours to strike where we were least expected. The area west of Tripoli was Gaddafi territory – firmly behind the front line – and contained the headquarters and barracks of 32 Brigade which we had encountered around Zlitan and Misrata. It was also a marshalling area for Gaddafi's heavy reserves and equipment and the

CAOC had identified a number of main battle tanks and armoured personnel carriers in a wood to the south of the barracks within 1,000m of the coast. The Apaches would be feet wet throughout and supported by a Predator, so this appeared to be a much less risky mission. The Predator–Apache combination was to pay real dividends. As the pair of Apaches approached the coast the UAV identified a truck-mounted radar siting right on the coast. The Apaches destroyed it with a single Hellfire and then silenced a number of Gaddafi troops who engaged the helicopters with small arms — a very poor decision. The way was now clear to find the tanks which were helpfully laser indicated by the Predator, and three were destroyed. The Apaches were back onboard *OCEAN* within 90 minutes of launching. After the previous strikes when we had taken on 32 Bde at its strongest — and been engaged by missiles as a result — this new approach seemed to offer a much greater prospect of achieving the psychological effect we were after. We were now hitting Gaddafi forces hard in their own backyard and the threat to our aircraft was reduced by the element of surprise gained by repositioning between missions.

Predator support had been key, but more often than not a UAV was not available, and the planned mission was cancelled as a result. This was also the case for 2 July and the next strike night was Sunday 3. This time the target was three vehicle check points blocking the road between Zuwara and Az-Zawiyah. Two pairs of Apaches were launched and effectively cleared the roads with nine Hellfire missiles. As before the only returned fire was from small arms which the Apaches silenced with 30mm.

We were now approaching the next full moon period and would be heading for Malta for a brief operational stand-off. For me, however, it would be far from a rest but a busy period in port. Not only would I be hosting visits from Rear Admiral Corder (COMOPS) and Major General Messenger from PJHQ, I also hoped to discover if my removal had been finally cancelled or simply delayed. Once the UK visit was over I would be joining Admiral Coindreau in travelling to Naples for a NATO commanders' conference. As we started heading towards Malta on 4 July I went into my usual Monday routine. I had a good phone call with Admiral Corder and then attended the Fleet Command Group by video conference. Out of the blue I received tasking direct from PJHQ to provide advice on the risk/reward balance for ongoing Apache operations – and thankfully had my previous draft ready to go. I amended it slightly to reflect the experience of the most recent strikes which showed how striking in different locations and UAV support could reduce risk and increase the effectiveness of Apache strikes. Wishing to ensure that Gary Waterfall and I were on the same page I forwarded the note to him – as the UK's Air Component Commander – to forward to PJHQ. My final call of the day was with the deputy NATO Maritime Component Commander Rear Admiral Jon Westbrook. I back-briefed him on my call on Admiral Foffi and my view that AH could make a significant contribution to increasing the pressure on the Gaddafi regime by contributing to maritime operations off the Libyan coast and striking the small boats that the regime employed. Admiral Foffi had said that he would take the idea forward but appeared very focused on maintaining the scheduled NATO shipping off the Libyan coast. Jon Westbrook was supportive – but not optimistic that the NATO maritime component would be able to think imaginatively about using air power – not helped by a reportedly strained relationship between the NATO Maritime Commander Vice Admiral Rinaldo in Naples and his Task Group Commander in *GARIBALDI*.

As we approached Malta, and firmly stood down from operations, I was able to host a small drinks party to celebrate the award of the Légion d'honneur to my French liaison officer Bernard Vettori and to say goodbye to two key members of staff who were departing. The first was my ATO and air power advisor Lieutenant Commander Paul Tremelling. Paul had done a first-class job in making those former amphibious warfare specialists in the team (including me) more aware of how air tasking and air space management worked – absolutely vital for integrating maritime strike into the larger air campaign. His replacement was the equally talented fellow Harrier pilot Lieutenant Commander Neil Twigg. The other leaver was my medical planner Lieutenant Commander Karen Duke. Karen had provided excellent medical advice throughout, ensuring that the needed NATO surgical support teams were always near enough to *OCEAN* to enable strikes to launch and plans were in place to deal with casualties. Her final act was to convince the UK to fly a surgical team to *OCEAN* – drawing military experts out of NHS roles to join the ship – and then ensuring their seamless integration into the ship with all the stores and equipment they might need. With the team about to become operational in *OCEAN* Karen's job was done and she could return the UK.

With the farewells complete I then welcomed Admiral Ian Corder onboard *OCEAN*. That evening the Admiral joined me and some selected staff for dinner in my cabin. *OCEAN* was showing its fragility and an air-conditioning plant was down, making it a very warm dinner indeed. It did enable me to highlight that conditions onboard were far from pleasant – especially for the deck crews moving around aircraft and carrying out maintenance. Indeed, you could not fail to be impressed by the support staff of the USAF 56th Rescue Squadron and the British Army teams of 25 Army Air Corps ground crew and 35 Aviation Technicians (led respectively by Doug Reid and Charlotte Joyce) who worked in demanding and unfamiliar conditions to ensure the aircraft were always ready to fly when called for. As an Army technician explained to me, in Afghanistan they might be required to fold/spread the rotors in an Apache once a week or so; in *OCEAN* it was a number of times a day, to get the helicopter from the hangar to the flight deck and back again. And the hangar was usually hot (even when the ACUs were working) and certainly cramped.

We arrived in Malta on 6 July and General Messenger and Group Captain Johnny Stringer (from PJHQ) and Gary Waterfall from the CAOC embarked to join Admiral Corder for briefings. My staff set the scene and I was able to use my risk/reward note as the script – in my view the risk to our people was very obvious and unavoidable but could be to some extent mitigated by fixed-wing and UAV support, careful planning and manoeuvring to ensure surprise. If we continued to strike into Libya we should be ready to lose an aircraft and accept the propaganda boon this would give the Gaddafi regime. The main question for PJHQ and indeed NATO was, did the psychological impact of AH operations outweigh this risk? The other factor that the Flag Captain stressed was the increasingly fragile state of *OCEAN* which needed a two-week maintenance period to sustain operations beyond the summer. The next day the visitors toured the ship and met all the key players. The result of the visit and briefings was that they agreed to review the AH contribution at the end of July but we should expect to be flying beyond that point.

General Messenger also took the opportunity to have a quiet word with me about my sacking. CJO had indeed been badly briefed but all were now clear that I was doing a good and vital job and that I would be needed as long as maritime strike operations continued... but don't expect a signal (formal order) to say any of that! It was a huge relief, and I took it as a vote of confidence not only in me but more importantly in my small team. The message was getting through that there was more to maritime strike than simply launching helicopters from a deck. A cloud was therefore lifted as my senior visitors departed and the next day I enjoyed a quiet 24 hours to recharge batteries and get a haircut.

★★

The break was only short. On Saturday 9 July I met up with Admiral Coindreau at Malta airport. The Admiral flew in by helicopter from *CHARLES DE GAULLE* and had very kindly invited me to join him in his French Navy plane for the flight to Naples and the NATO Command Conference. It was a real pleasure to be back in his company – not only did we get on well, we faced very similar challenges in delivering a national capability to the NATO campaign and both shared the very keen awareness of the risks our helicopter crews were taking. Being in Naples enabled me to catch up with the key British officers within the NATO structure – Rear Admiral Russ Harding (Deputy Joint Commander) and Rear Admiral Jon Westbrook (Deputy Maritime Component Commander). It was clear that the Task Group's efforts – and the important effect the attack helicopter strikes were having on pro-Gaddafi forces' minds — were fully recognised in the NATO HQ.

The Command Conference itself took place on the Sunday and brought into sharp focus the divides between the national and coalition effort. I had by now sat through countless UK (Fleet and PJHQ) video meetings where NATO was hardly mentioned at all — the impression being that this was a UK effort (Operation *Ellamy*) rather than a contribution to a NATO one (Operation *Unified Protector*) that provided the strategic leadership for the campaign.

The reverse was true at the NATO HQ where the focus was absolutely the coalition effort. The attendance itself was in itself very revealing. The Joint Commander, Charles Bouchard, hosted, the other key participants being the Air Component Commander (Lieutenant General Joddice), Admiral Coindreau and me. National card holders and national representatives such as Gary Waterfall were excluded — this was a very select group. Admiral Sam Lockear also addressed us, making it clear that the US was supporting operations from behind the scenes.

The sense of the meeting was a concern that despite the considerable efforts so far there was a real danger of stalemate — with few advances by the rebels and no concessions by Gaddafi. Although the rebels, now known as the Free Libyan Forces (FLF), had, with the benefit of NATO strikes, seen off the Gaddafi offensive around Misrata the front lines appeared to be largely static — to the west of Benghazi in the east, around Misrata and south of Zuwarah in vicinity of the Nafusa mountains. This was linked to a worry that August would solidify this position with NATO leave and Ramadan combining to create a period of inactivity. Therefore, the remainder of July represented a key opportunity to make progress. The role of AH in increasing the pressure on the regime was discussed — and the French and UK Task Group's efforts applauded. In turn, I was able to highlight the key role of UAVs in both providing targets for attack helicopters and of course reducing the risk to the aircrew. However, since UAVs were in short supply — there were often only three UAV tasking lines across the whole of Libya — we needed to limit our expectations. General Bouchard also said that he felt the NATO mission would extend well beyond the summer – either to continue to put pressure on the regime, or if Gaddafi fell, to prepare for the arrival of a stabilisation force.

It was an excellent meeting, bringing together the commanders and aligning our thinking which was invaluable. It was also a pleasure to be free of some of the politics within the UK system and to have the confidence of those leading the coalition effort.

The next day I was back in HMS *OCEAN* heading back towards Libya. With General Bouchard's and Messenger's advice to be prepared for a prolonged operation I had my staff work on a note exploring how we might extend the AH effort into the autumn and beyond. In terms of staff this was doable since the *ALBION* group with the majority of my staff would be back in the UK in early August. I therefore asked Tom Guy, in *ALBION,* to work up a roulemont plan to keep the right size staff off Libya into 2012. In terms of shipping the key would be bringing *ILLUSTRIOUS* out of refit in time to replace *OCEAN*, again in early 2012. It was all doable and it made sense to start the planning now.

It being a Monday the first serial was the Fleet Command Group. I was able to brief the meeting on the NATO Command Conference and the high regard shown for the UK and French Task Group's efforts. I gave a heads-up that I was looking how we might sustain our efforts into the New Year. Looking slightly ahead I mentioned that we should consider using the *ALBION* group's return to the Mediterranean on 23 July to strengthen the messaging against the Gaddafi regime. This was timely since we had just received further intelligence that the Gaddafi regime was still expecting, and indeed preparing for, a NATO amphibious assault in the vicinity of Brega. In my mind this was a result of the continuing French focus on the area and the presence of French (and in early June UK) assault ships.

OCEAN was now at the peak of its capability. In addition to our tailored air group of five Apache, two Sea King ASAC and Lynx helicopters, the three USAF HH-60G Pave Hawks provided organic combat search and rescue and our newly embarked surgical team our own ability to deal with serious casualties. Positioning within flight times of NATO ships' medical facilities was no longer a limiting factor to where we might operate. The surgical team were an impressive tri-service bunch commanded by vascular surgeon, Surgeon Commander Peter Taylor. He was supported by consultant anaesthetist Surgeon Commander Shane McCabe, Army theatre nurse Major Mike Berski, critical care nurse Petty Officer Claire Williams, RAF emergency department nurse Corporal Suzi Smith and biomedical scientist Warrant Officer Beccy Hatch. The speed with which they integrated into the ship and the enthusiasm they showed for the task was a huge credit to them all – and indeed *OCEAN*'s small medical team that hosted them. *OCEAN* was demonstrating how effective maritime strike could be.

The strike on 11 July was against the same vehicle check points we had hit on 3 July blocking the road between Zuwara and Az-Zawiyah. Surveillance suggested that check points had been rebuilt and needed striking. Returning to the same target – albeit a week later – carried the obvious risk of flying against an enemy that was prepared for attack or, worse, flying into a full-blown ambush. To reduce the risk we decided to launch much later than normal, with a strike window of 0230–0400, and to approach the target from an unexpected direction – from the desert rather than directly from the sea. As the Apaches crossed the coast two pro-Gaddafi troops were seen to take up firing positions and were silenced. The Apache then flew on 26km to strike two vehicle check points whose defences were seen to be pointing in the direction of the coast – which the AH had carefully avoided. Eleven Hellfires and 500 rounds of 30mm cleared the check points. As they returned, near the coast a pro-Gaddafi position – three technicals including one with a barrelled weapon on the back – was also destroyed.

The 12 July was mixed. There were hopes that our scarcity of UAVs might be offset by gaining situational awareness from the ground via better communications with the FLF and their supporters. Apaches would effectively be placed on deck alert and respond to any targets that were identified. By 1800 no targets had been spotted and yet by 2100 we began to receive reports of a number of potential missions. A

Predator UAV was bought onto task to look into the identified areas and during my Go/No Go brief confirmed that they contained no suitable targets. Unsurprisingly the strike was cancelled. The next day I spoke to Gary Waterfall on the subject and we both shared the same concern about attack helicopters being held at deck alert to respond to emerging targets without the benefit of persistent, reliable surveillance.

We now entered five days of high light levels that precluded Apache strikes. The opportunity was taken to carry out maintenance on the ship and helicopters and for some rest for the aircrews and ship's company. For me it meant a few days of actually sleeping during the night rather than being in the operations room waiting for the Apaches and Sea King to return. I was very conscious of how these working patterns and the daily strain of authorising strikes were affecting me – and how tired it was easy to become. Being the Commodore meant that I spent a lot of time on my own in my cabin/office (a privilege in a packed busy ship) and I gave plenty of time to think about what we were doing – a vital part of command. I was braced throughout for the moment that we might lose aircraft and people and knew that when the moment came – like the fire in *PURSUER* – all eyes would be on me. I therefore prepared my thoughts for how I would handle this when it happened. And no one could not be affected by the gun tapes that the Apaches brought back from every mission that vividly brought to life the consequences of the Go decision that I gave at the evening briefing. I had no doubt about the legality or reasoning of our mission and thanks to all my previous roles had confidence in myself and my decisions. I saw my role as very much protecting the ships and aircrew from the politics that I was often engaged with and the various frictions between NATO, national and service organisations. Hence my decision to keep my sacking (now rescinded) from the staff.

In terms of the mission and how we operated I sought and welcomed the views of all of the team and used both Al Livingstone (Chief of Staff) and Andy Betton (Flag Captain) as sounding boards for my ideas and concerns. But of course I kept a great deal to myself. One evening as I sat in my cabin there was a knock at the cabin door and there was Bernard Clarke, HMS *OCEAN*'s Chaplain. The naval chaplain is different from those in the other services since they wear no rank but by convention assume the rank of the person they are speaking to. This gives them the great advantage of speaking freely to everyone onboard. Bernard came in and asked for a chat. Since it was a non-strike night I offered him a drink and we began to talk. 'I notice,' he said 'the seriousness of what you do every night and wanted to ask if you are OK?' It was a generous, insightful and, I discovered as he said it, welcome question. I was able to thank him for his care and concern and reassure him that I fully appreciated what I was doing and was comfortable doing it — thanks to having thought about the legal basis and the nature of the mission a great deal. Here was the naval chaplaincy at its best — showing concern for all on board, including me, and on reflection passing the message that those in *OCEAN* appreciated what I was doing. It really helped.

During this operational pause we received the warning order to be prepared to remain on task until April 2012. We were clearly getting ready to deal with a prolonged campaign. The staff had, before the first strike, completed their own assessment of how the campaign might unfold and my intelligence staff were carefully looking for signs of success. To us it seemed that there would be three indicators. Firstly, the nations adjacent to Libya would come down on the side of the FLF — in other words they were no longer convinced that the Gaddafi regime would survive. Then we might expect to see the mercenaries that he employed deciding that fighting the FLF was no longer a sensible business model. Finally, we thought that the end would be close when Gaddafi's own family members abandoned him and fled. By mid-July it was clear that Gaddafi was indeed losing the support of his neighbours and on 16 July we noticed the FLF front in the west beginning to advance towards Brega. Maybe this was the beginning of the end.

Also, on 16 July the Type 23 frigate HMS *IRON DUKE* arrived in the Joint Operating Area. It was returning to the UK at the end of a Gulf deployment and would briefly replace HMS *LIVERPOOL* in the NATO Task Group. The commanding officer Commander

Nick Cooke-Priest came across to the flagship for briefings by the staff – and made a very positive first impression. With our excellent Operational Intelligence Support Cell we were able to provide the latest operational picture and carried on providing this support to Nick throughout his time off Libya. Like *LIVERPOOL* the *IRON DUKE* was to operate off Misrata – and successfully used its 4.5in gun to destroy a pro-Gaddafi gun battery before handing the duty back to the destroyer.

The 18 July saw us ready to recommence AH strikes to the west of Misrata. Being a Monday it involved the usual calls and meetings. Prior to the Fleet Command Group I spoke to both Admirals Harding and Westbrook to gain a sense of the current constraints on the NATO campaign. There was a particular focus on *OCEAN* since it was the only high-readiness maritime strike platform on task, since *CHARLES DE GAULLE* was alongside in Crete for maintenance and the helicopter carrier *TONNERRE* had handed over to *MISTRAL* which would not be ready for operations until 27 July. The absence of the French carrier also meant a reduction in tactical reconnaissance capability at a time when movement was being detected on all fronts. General Bouchard was clear that in terms of surveillance Tripoli (the capital) remained the priority so the prospect of persistent surveillance to enable and support AH strikes was not encouraging. There was a hope, still to be proved, that our awareness of the ground might improve as FLF advanced into Gaddafi territory. The Sea King ASAC was however really demonstrating its ability to provide an important contribution to the coalition's ground surveillance effort – and particularly the ability to detect and track moving vehicles. I also passed on my continuing request for the NATO Task Group Commander in *GARIBALDI* to provide details of PGF patterns of life in order to cue AH strikes against Gaddafi small boats. I briefed all this to the Fleet meeting – chaired on this occasion by the Second Sea Lord Vice Admiral Charles Montgomery. Looking into the future, *OCEAN* would have an operational stand-down in Malta on 10–17 August (when the evenings would be too bright to strike) and I said if needed I would start changing over my staff in October and that I was working on the detail of how we might extend maritime strike into 2012. Unsurprisingly given the paucity of persistent surveillance and in particular UAVs the evening's strike was cancelled.

On 19 July we were back attacking the rear areas of 32 Brigade and the targets were two large buildings in which main battle tanks were believed to be stored, 5 miles west of Zlitan. The targets were within 2 miles of the coast — but to ensure surprise the pilots chose an indirect approach that would see them attacking from the south i.e. the opposite direction from the coast. This was very much the area in which the NATO Task Group was also active, and HMS *LIVERPOOL* was tasked to fire star shell into the area prior to our attack. Fired from the ship's 4.5in gun, the shell releases a flare that hangs under a parachute and turns night into day over the target area. Clearly this would put the Apaches in danger so *LIVERPOOL'*s task was due to end 20 minutes before the Apaches made their approach. With everything in place the Go decision was given and two Apaches launched.

As they approached the coast it was evident that *LIVERPOOL* was still firing, beyond its mission end time, so they called *OCEAN'*s operation room to ask us to get *LIVERPOOL* to stop. The ATO was clear the airspace into which *LIVERPOOL* was firing was now allocated to the Apaches and at best it would delay their arrival over the target; at worst it would reveal their presence to 32 Brigade. The principal warfare officer (PWO) in *OCEAN* called up his opposite number in the destroyer and told him to cease firing. *LIVERPOOL'*s PWO, clearly caught up in the moment, came back with a negative and continued to engage. It was an occasion to pull rank and on the radio circuit from *OCEAN* came: 'From COMUKTG you are to check fire [cease firing] immediately.' The use of my callsign had the desired effect and the star shelling ceased.

The Apaches continued. On reaching the coast they detected two individuals who appeared to be on look-out over the coast. A burst of 30mm saw them running for their lives and as always the pilots displayed their knowledge of the Rules of Engagement and let them go on their way. Navigating inland — and avoiding myriad power cables strung between electricity pylons – they approached the target building as planned and fired 10 Hellfire missiles into them. Our intelligence had been right in that the area became alive with PGF troops – this clearly was an important military location. As the Apaches departed a further Hellfire destroyed the vehicle check point protecting the site.

In the remainder of the week another three strikes were conducted against 32 Brigade facilities in or near Zlitan. For the first time co-ordinated strikes were conducted with RAF Typhoon and Tornado aircraft – with fast jet attacks being followed up by Apaches. On 21 July this saw a building complex near the coast effectively destroyed. The 21st also saw reports of a FLF attack on the Sheraton Hotel in Tripoli in which a number of PGF leaders had either been killed or wounded. This was the first significant report I had seen of armed resistance in the capital – maybe Gaddafi's hold on power was slipping.

We were in a routine of striking every other night and it was important that I continued to think about how we could sustain strikes and the morale of the men and women who were delivering them – and that included all in *OCEAN*. In June we had already heard the disappointing news that those in *OCEAN* would not qualify for operational allowance since we were routinely operating outside of Libyan territorial waters. We were of course launching strikes from approximately 20 miles offshore – and the conditions in *OCEAN* were, due to frequently failing air conditioning units, far from comfortable. The Army personnel found the decision the hardest to accept but as always we simply focused on the job. We were a very mixed bunch; excluding the USAF we had we had Navy, Army and Royal Air Force personnel, all with different terms and conditions of service.

These differences were brought into sharp focus by the way in which the Services approached the upcoming operational stand-down period in August and a longer planned maintenance period in September. Army and RAF personnel were entitled to return home for a week or so at public expense whereas Navy personnel, including Royal Marines, were not entitled to this but could get an interest-free loan to fly families out to join them in the Mediterranean.

This seemed unfair and indeed divisive to a team that were working seamlessly together.

At the evening command brief I announced that I intended to write and request that everyone in *OCEAN* received the same package – of travel to and from the UK at Crown expense and an interest-free loan to enable families to fly out. The logistics lead in *OCEAN*, and therefore my staff lead, told me that there was no point in writing such a letter since the existing rules were very clear. I acknowledged what the current rules said but I still wanted to ask for new arrangements – after all the three services had never been thrown together in these circumstances before. The staff lead pushed back twice more – there was, in his view, no point raising the issue and eventually, slightly exasperated, I asked the Flag Captain to draft the letter. Suffice to say the note was forwarded to Paul Abraham in Northwood on 22 July and six days later the new arrangements came into effect. It proved how much support we were getting from the Fleet HQ and PJHQ – and the adage that if you don't ask you don't get!

On 22 July my liaison officer to the NATO CTG in *GARIBALDI*, Lieutenant Commander Steve Wren, returned to *OCEAN*. He described an afloat HQ which had transitioned from running NATO Operation *Active Endeavour* – monitoring the movement of merchant ships in the Mediterranean – to enforcing an arms embargo on Libya without shifting from a peacetime to war footing. Despite the assurances of Admiral Foffi, the idea of using AH to raise the pressure on Gaddafi had found no traction with his staff. One to raise in my next call with Admiral Westbrook – but I sensed a missed opportunity.

The 23 July saw the Task Group reformed as *OCEAN* and *FORT ROSALIE* were joined by *ALBION* and *SUTHERLAND* and the tanker *ORANGELEAF*. Commander Roger Readwin came across early to call and was as upbeat and enthusiastic as ever – and keen to contribute in any way he could to the mission. I would have *SUTHERLAND* with me for just over a week and would use it for force protection of *OCEAN*, naval gunfire support and to broadcast positive NATO messaging to the people of Libya via a capability known as radio in a box. That evening we launched a two-Apache mission against a military complex to the south of Zlitan and *SUTHERLAND* provided protection for *OCEAN* as we closed the coast.

On Saturday 24 July I went across to *ALBION* to see Captain James Morley, his heads of department and the majority of my staff who had stayed with *ALBION*. James had done a first-class job leading the amphibious elements of the RFTG east of Suez and I wanted him and his team to know what an important and successful job they had done in achieving the strategic aim of the *Cougar* deployment – strengthening links in the Middle East and enabling me to focus on Libya. I was also able to point out that Gaddafi had wasted time and resources continuing to build defences against an expected amphibious assault around Brega: a real demonstration of one of the effects that Amphibious Task Groups can create without conducting landings. It was a slightly sad final visit to *ALBION* since the Fleet flagship role would be handed over to its sister *BULWARK* in the autumn and this would be *ALBION*'s final outing before going into extended readiness. The ship's company that I had helped build in my previous role as its captain, and had enjoyed working with as the commodore, would break up and move onto new ships and establishments.

I had similar messages for my staff, who had done well supporting Captain James in *ALBION* and providing staff horsepower to me in *OCEAN*. The chief of staff, Commander Tom Guy, had juggled this with style. His focus now was on how we might maintain a staff off Libya into the autumn and beyond and so getting those in *ALBION* home for some leave and then back to relieve the *OCEAN* team was a priority. I also said goodbye to two stars of my staff who had remained in *ALBION* but were now moving to new roles. Lieutenant Commander Tim Neild who was the staff operations officer and therefore Tom's right-hand man was moving on to well-deserved promotion to commander and I was also losing First Officer Tony Day. Tony was a Royal Fleet Auxiliary Officer who had the rare knack of producing stores ships and tankers just as they were needed and therefore kept the Task Group at sea. I returned to *OCEAN* in time to meet Captain Paul Lloyd – an old friend and now Captain Surface Ships with the Devonport Flotilla with responsibility for the

Plymouth-based frigates, like *SUTHERLAND*, and for keeping a watching brief for me over *BULWARK* while I was away. This was a chance for me to sing *SUTHERLAND*'s praises and to hear that Paul felt that Captain Alex Burton was on track to bring *BULWARK* back to the fleet on time. I also got some feedback on how the RFTG was being seen at home. It was all positive.

Monday 25 July's Fleet Command Group saw me raise the need for an organic maritime UAV to enable us to provide the much-needed surveillance capability to cue strikes without depending on scarce NATO Predators. *OCEAN* and *ALBION* had the ability to receive the down link from UAVs but we simply didn't have any in the UK orbat. Another COMUKTG note resulted — in the short term other nations might provide UAVs to the mission and in the longer term the MOD might procure some for HM ships. I was also able to report that the new French Helicopter Strike Group was now operational in the helicopter carrier *MISTRAL*. They had conducted a relatively straightforward strike and were planning to commence operations in earnest around Brega that evening. Finally, I mentioned that I was about to detach *ALBION* and send it on its way back to the UK. I suggested that Fleet/UK might want to consider what role it or *BULWARK*, and indeed the RFTG, could or might play in subsequent operations in Libya (including after the conflict ended). Beyond my pay grade but worth thinking about, especially since I was monitoring the handover between *ALBION* and *BULWARK*. After the meeting I had a phone call with Admiral Westbrook who agreed to support the case for maritime UAVs and to put pressure on Admiral Foffi to produce parameters for maritime AH operations. Our strike for the evening was cancelled — again due to lack of surveillance capability — and *SUTHERLAND* declared its 4.5in gun defective, much to my and Roger Readwin's frustration.

At about the same time I had an interesting conversation with the commanding officer of the embarked Sea King ASAC. There was no question that the ASAC was making a tremendous contribution to the coalition surveillance effort of the airspace above and ground in Libya. The CO questioned the current C2 arrangement by which the aircraft worked for me primarily to provide early warning to protect *OCEAN*, with spare capacity going to the coalition surveillance effort. He felt it would be more appropriate for aircraft to be tasked by the Joint Commander with any spare capacity being provided back to me for force protection. It was an interesting proposition that I rejected since the lack of a dedicated escort left me dependent on NATO units that might not always be available. A few days later we received intelligence from satellite imagery that the PGF had removed a number of anti-ship missile launchers from stricken Libyan warships in Tripoli harbour. At the evening command brief I reminded the staff of the use of a land-based Exocet missile by Argentina in 1982 to hit the British destroyer HMS *GLAMORGAN*. The same threat was now present for us and I was relieved that I had kept first call on the Sea Kings.

As expected, the tempo of AH strikes reduced as NATO's surveillance assets were stretched over three active fronts and Tripoli. The planned strikes on the 27 and 28 July were cancelled, although on 28 July the aircraft were, having been stood down, rapidly prepared to launch in response to intelligence indicating the movement of PGF main battle tanks. The suspected area attracted Predator support but no targets were seen and the strike was finally cancelled (again!).

The 28 July also saw the publishing of MOD instruction dealing with the compulsory redundancies resulting from the recent Strategic Defence and Security Review. The note was well intentioned in that it aimed to exempt those involved in active operations from the round – but unfortunately it described those on Libya operations as being those within 12nm of the Libyan coast. That morning's operations group conference with Admiral Corder established that this was an oversight that would be quickly corrected – much go the relief of my sailors, marines, soldiers and airmen.

Friday 29 July was a maintenance day followed by a rest day on the Saturday – including a flight deck barbecue on *OCEAN*. Access to the flight deck on a busy helicopter or aircraft carrier is a real treat for all onboard. Understandably gaining access during operational days can be difficult but I would always try to get onto the flight deck to run a couple of times a week. My military assistant, Lieutenant

Andy Parker, would carefully check the flying programme and get the relevant permissions before I would appear. The keen runners onboard soon cottoned on to the fact that I was probably the only runner who would not be loudly ordered off the flight deck and I would soon be joined by a string of people enjoying the exercise. To have the *OCEAN* team – Army, Navy, Air Force and USAF – on deck for some relaxation and to enjoy the ship's band was a real highlight.

On the last day of July I flew across to *SUTHERLAND* to thank the ship's company for all they had done in the RFTG before I sent them on their way. After discussions with the ever-enthusiastic Roger Readwin I visited the chief petty officers' mess, had lunch with the heads of department, visited the operations room and the galley – in which you can find the gossip in any ship – and a junior rates' mess. Morale was very high – as you would expect from such a well-led ship that had done a great job both east of Suez and in the Mediterranean and was about to head home. The final serial was a glass of champagne to celebrate the achievements of *SUTHERLAND*'s flight commander while the ship was replenishing from *FORT ROSALIE*. I said my farewells and flew back to *OCEAN* – managing to get some great photographs of *SUTHERLAND*, *FORT ROSALIE* and *ORANGELEAF* replenishing.

That evening's strike was later than normal and was in close co-operation with fast jets. The target was Al-Khums port in between Tripoli and Misrata, enabling the Apaches to remain largely over the sea as the fast jets struck buildings within the harbour. The plan was for the helicopters to strike any PGF military response to the air strikes. None was seen so the Apaches returned to *OCEAN* without engaging.

Monday 1 August was both a normal Fleet Command Group (FCG) day but more importantly for Libya and the Arab world it was the start of Ramadan. Despite this, fighting continued on the ground, particularly around Zlitan and Brega, but as yet no major PGF breakthrough had been made and the Gaddafi regime continued in its efforts to discredit the uprising and NATO's efforts in the media. The FCG was chaired by the Deputy Commander in Chief, Vice Admiral George Zambellas. He was to be in the chair for August and opened with the clear message that while operations were ongoing the Fleet Headquarters would not be going on leave. His support for both the Group and me personally could not have been clearer. The other issue that was keeping the Fleet Headquarters busy was the recently announced restructuring of the top level of Defence. The service chiefs would be removed from the Defence Management Board and be 'rusticated', spending more time at their service headquarters than in London. The single-service commanders in chief would be removed, and new arrangements developed over the summer.

I briefed the Group on the Al Khums strike and explained that the paucity of surveillance assets was now very directly impacting on the tempo of operations. We had only flown one mission in seven days with five being cancelled due to the lack of cueing/targets. Today we had a strike planned in the vicinity of Zlitan and would be flying Sea King ASAC in support of the NATO maritime component. I was able to report that the French Helicopter Strike Group in *MISTRAL* was now fully operational and that the French focus remained very much the Brega front. Finally, I said that I had visited *SUTHERLAND* and was about to detach it for home and I once again sang the ship's praises. The rest of the day continued as per normal – and rather predictably the evening's strike was cancelled due to the lack of surveillance assets.

Tuesday was planned to be a strike day. The staff were working on how the group (both Apache and SKASAC) might work better with NATO Maritime Patrol Aircraft and were refining the long list of lessons identified we had been compiling since leaving the UK – they would form the basis of the Post Deployment Report that we would soon be drafting. During the day I also said goodbye to Admiral Coindreau's liaison officer, Lieutenant Colonel Bernard Vettori. Bernard had done a first-class job. While I would speak to the French admiral on a regular basis Bernard was talking to him and his staffs several times a day and the two groups were always in step as a result. Bernard's replacement was Lieutenant Colonel Valerie Bermond who fitted seamlessly into the team.

That evening's target was a 32 Brigade ammunition and weapons storage facility located in a beach hotel complex. The plan would see fast jets striking with Paveway guided bombs from 25,000ft and the Apaches from low level, remaining over the sea throughout. The Apaches struck first, firing their Hellfires at discrete targets within the compound. This was followed by a Paveway from the fast jets that left a single storage container unscathed, which in turn was destroyed by Hellfires. Forty-five minutes after launching the Apaches safely returned to *OCEAN*.

★★

The strike planned for Wednesday 3 August was cancelled. I spent some of the day peace-making between Gary Waterfall (UK Air Component Commander) and Rear Admiral Westbrook over HMS *LIVERPOOL*. The previous evening *LIVERPOOL* had been engaging a target with its 4.5in gun in an area where the Targeting Directive placed restrictions on non-precision fires — such as naval gunfire support. The air battle was being co-ordinated on behalf of the Air Component Commander by an airborne controller — usually in a command and control aircraft. The controller asked *LIVERPOOL* to check fire and after some convincing it did. Gary Waterfall rightly passed his concern to me, as his friendly sailor, and I was able to explain the difficult NATO command and control structure that *LIVERPOOOL* found itself in and perhaps the lack of direction and guidance it was getting from its own NATO Task Group. I said I would speak to Rear Admiral Westbrook within the NATO Maritime Component Command and to *LIVERPOOL* to ensure the lesson was learnt. It seemed to me important not to blow this out of proportion — the key message for *LIVERPOOL* was that if the Air Component Commander asked you to check fire your 4.5in you should do so — unless you were retuning fire to a position that was firing at you.

Thursday 4 August was a busy day, even for me. The morning Fleet 'O group' video teleconference was chaired by Rear Admiral Ian Corder and went well. Thereafter, the NATO CTG Rear Admiral Foffi visited. The usual round of briefings was held and the Admiral continued to say all the right things. An important discussion point for me remained utilising the *OCEAN* group to support the wider NATO maritime effort. We agreed to see if we could use the Sea King ASACs' excellent ground surveillance capability to cue Maritime Patrol Aircraft onto targets where their advanced infra-red cameras could cue strikes.

That evening's strikes were a major change for us. So far we had joined the French in their efforts around Brega in the east and had operated against the PGF forces in and around Misrata and Zlitan in the west. We were now going to operate against the third FLF/PGF front line some 50 miles inland (south-west of Tripoli) towards the Nafusa mountains. The target was a position near the town of Bi'r Al Ghanam where PFG military equipment was believed to be present along with a number of vehicle check points along what was known as Main Supply Route Gold that ran out of the town. This would be our longest-range strike, some 20nm from the ships to the coast then a further 50 miles to the strike and back again. The Apache teams in *OCEAN* together with the planning cell in the CAOC worked up the plan and got it through the CAOC and into the ATO. The CAOC's Go decision brought the mission to us and with the important element of surprise on our side I too gave a Go at the evening decision meeting.

A strike package of two attack helicopters was launched, with the usual Sea King and fast jet support. Having crossed the coastline the Apaches were soon over open desert and then approaching Bi'r Al Ghanam. At the first target position the Apaches detected nothing and moved on to the first vehicle check point where the main road to Tripoli intersected the road to the town of Az-Zawiyah. Here a well-found VCP was detected and destroyed, together with two vehicles, by 30mm gun. At the second VCP a Hellfire missile was used to destroy the target and a vehicle, and the Apaches set off for home. As they approached the coast they detected a further VCP with a great deal of activity around it – including five vehicles. This VCP had not been authorised by the CAOC as a pre-designated target so the Apaches manoeuvred over the sea and asked the air co-ordinator's permission to strike what was after all a fleeting target. With permission granted the Apaches made their approach. The PGF may have heard the Apaches as they made their first pass towards the sea and the vehicles were now scattered under trees in an attempt to hide them – confirming their status as valid targets. The first Hellfire missile saw the PGF troops abandoning both their positions and vehicles which were then destroyed.

As per normal the team onboard *OCEAN* went through the mission's gun tapes and discovered two main battle tanks in the first target area that had not been seen by the aircrew. That said, the tanks had no heat source and may have not been serviceable – and this did not lessen the success of what had been one of our best missions. It is difficult to assess the impact of the individual AH strikes but it would have now been clear to the Gaddafi regime that all the front lines were liable to no-notice precision Apache strikes. What is more, the news of these first Apache strikes on the Nafusa mountains – or south-west front – may have encouraged the rebels to go on the offensive and weakened the PGF's resolve, and in the next 48 hours we began to see real movement in this area.

After four hours' sleep I was back into the strike day routine. A routine battle staff video conference, chaired by Rear Admiral Duncan Potts, took the morning but in the afternoon the focus was on our next planned strike against more VCPs on the Nafusa front. But things were now beginning to move. We received unconfirmed FLF reports that Gaddafi's son and commander of 32 Brigade had been killed and the strike was cancelled since the intended targets, once firmly in PGF hands, were now contested by the FLF. On Saturday 6 August the FLF advanced over 10km and captured Bi'r Al Ghanam, with it threatening the key Gaddafi supply routes that we had struck two nights before. The stalemate was finally over.

In *OCEAN* Saturday began with a moment of reflection with a memorial service for Lieutenant Joshua Woodhouse who had sadly died a year before in an accident onboard while the ship was alongside in Mayport, Florida. Joshua was a popular member of *OCEAN* and I recalled the impact his death had had – both in *OCEAN* and in the wider group of which I had been a part in *ALBION* at the time. The service was extremely moving and reflected how well Joshua was regarded and missed by his shipmates. I spent some valuable time talking to *OCEAN* sailors – who were looking forward to the next well-deserved operational stand-down and a maintenance period in September. They clearly understood the importance of what we were doing and had settled well into the strike routine and, in stark contrast to two months earlier, now fully embraced the uncertainty of operations. As a tired commodore I always found talking to servicemen and women – and their particular sense of humour and fun – an excellent tonic!

The staff were cautiously optimistic about the news coming from the FLF and certainly buoyed by the success and apparent impact of the previous strike. Saturday was another strike day and importantly it was planned to be on the now very active south-west front. The targets were to be in the vicinity of the Gaddafi-held Okba airfield. The airfield had been previously struck by fast jets and although its aircraft and anti-air defences had been destroyed it remained an important staging point for Gaddafi forces advancing to meet the rebels in the Nafusa mountains. It sat on the road from the mountains to Zuwara on the coast and striking it would both disrupt Gaddafi's reserves and, by clearing VCPs, open another route for a FLF advance. The strike would not be supported by a UAV but since Okba was well behind Gaddafi lines any military activity would be valid targets.

The target area was some 40 miles inland and the two Apaches approached along a main supply route where they came across 10 vehicles (six with weapons mounted on the back) adjacent to a VCP. The Apaches selected a clearly empty technical to hit first – to give the Gaddafi troops in the area a chance to get away from their vehicles. A second Hellfire and 30mm rounds followed and eight technicals were destroyed. The convoy destroyed, the Apaches pressed on towards the airfield which being only 5 miles away would have heard the explosions at the previous target. At the airfield itself the Apache crews saw a number of PGF troops in a defensive trench – and destroyed it with a Hellfire and 30mm before moving on to destroy four vehicles and a command and control node with a satellite dish receiver. By now the airfield was alive with PGF forces but the AH were at the point where their remaining fuel meant they had to begin their return to *OCEAN*. On the way back and still over the interior of Libya the AH were probably at their most vulnerable – high speed at low height with little fuel and ammunition remaining. On this night the alertness of one the Apache crew probably saved the aircraft since he spotted in his infra-red camera the tell-tale heat source of a manned weapon system on the back of a truck hidden in a group of trees 2km ahead (and at 120 knots that's close). A rapidly actioned Hellfire took out the threat. Just over two hours after launching both AHs safely recovered into *OCEAN* and we opened from the Libyan coast.

Sunday turned out to be a relatively quiet day, onboard *OCEAN* at least. Ashore Gaddafi's position was deteriorating as the FLF made progress on every front. In the south-west the FLF had continued their advance beyond Bi'r Al Ghanam and were now within 18km of the coast near the town of Surnam, mid-way between Tripoli and Zuwara. In Misrata the FLF managed to advance south into Tawaergha from where the regime had fired many of its indirect weapons into the enclave, and in the east the rebels launched an attempt to take New Brega to the east of the old town. The fluidity of the front line positions meant that without persistent surveillance assets like UAVS it would be increasingly difficult for Apaches to operate. In the contested areas both the FLF and PGF were operating similar vehicles (technicals) and above all else we had to avoid striking FLF forces in error. The priority for surveillance remained, quite rightly, Tripoli. A planned strike in the vicinity of Zlitan became deck alert with the crews ready to go, waiting for cueing from ashore. None came and they did not fly. Meanwhile the staff worked on a note for the CAOC and Gary Waterfall on how we might work with Maritime Patrol Aircraft.

Monday 8 August was a normal Fleet Command Group Day with *OCEAN* heading towards Malta for its next luminosity-driven operational stand-down. I reported the highly successful strikes on the south-western front and how I was exploring how we might be able to combine Maritime Patrol Aircraft with SKASAC to cue future AH strikes. I was also able – thanks to my excellent links with Admiral Coindreau – to inform Fleet about the sudden withdrawal of the

French aircraft carrier *CHARLES DE GAULLE*. Admiral Coindreau was himself surprised by the decision, taken in Paris but driven by the nuclear maintenance requirements of the carrier. It reminded me of an early discussion I had had with the Admiral. We were talking about the utility and value of aircraft carriers when he said, 'If you are going to have them make sure you have two – with only one you can guarantee when you need her most she will be in refit.' It meant that the Admiral would transfer many of his 50 staff to the helicopter carrier *MISTRAL* which already had a sizable Helicopter Strike Group staff embarked on about 10 August.

That evening my staff and I watched the TV footage of the riots in London and other English cities. I found it very sad and more than a little ironic that here we were risking lives to protect the people of Libya and give them a chance of gaining democracy while at home – one of the homes of democracy – widespread disorder was taking place.

OCEAN and *FORT ROSALIE* went alongside in Malta on 9 August and we did not return to sea until 17 August. For me this was a welcome chance to recharge batteries and spend some time with my wife Alison and my two daughters who flew out to join me.

In Libya the rebels continued to make progress. On 13 August they began a battle to seize the town of Gharyan, 80km south of Tripoli, which fell into their hands within two days. On the same day Az-Zawiyah, on the coast 47 km west of Tripoli, also fell. For Gaddafi this combination was a double blow – his forces in the south-west were now effectively isolated from the capital and losing Az-Zawiyah meant losing access to both the Tunisian border and two of the most important oil refineries in Libya. And on 16 August Gaddafi's Interior Minister Nasser Mabrouk Abdullah was the latest in a number of high-level defections when he and his family arrived in Egypt.

The French announced the withdrawal of their aircraft carrier but President Sarkozy visited the ship and made it clear that despite its departure 'France is committed to seeing the mission through'.[1] The net appeared to be closing on Gaddafi and the focus was shifting towards Tripoli. For the NATO air campaign the challenge was targeting ground targets in such a dynamic and contested battle space without the benefit of our own ground forces and spotters. This was highlighted by the destruction of what appeared to be a PGF main battle tank that had in fact been captured and was in FLF hands. NATO had little option but to tighten the rules regarding and the approval processes for strikes.

So it felt as if Libya was approaching a tipping point when *OCEAN* returned to sea on 17 August. By 19 August we were back off the Libyan coast when Gaddafi issued orders for his forces to fall back to the capital – the final showdown was clearly approaching. We conducted our first trial with a French Navy Atlantique Maritime Patrol Aircraft (MPA) working with our own Sea King ASAC to provide cueing for AH. The Sea King would use its radar to detect ground movement and vector the MPA onto the target where the MPA's camera could provide the required awareness for Apache strikes. It worked in theory but unfortunately the MPA stayed at very high altitude and did not close within 20nm – and its camera was not up to the job.

Saturday 20 August was a key day in the downfall of Gaddafi regime with the FLF launching the battle to take Tripoli. Rebels advanced along the coast road to the west and uprisings took place in a number of the capital's districts. Overnight heavy fighting was reported in the city with the regime attempting to suppress protests with heavy weapons and snipers. Gaddafi also tried to reinforce his units within the city by moving artillery and armour into the city. In *OCEAN* we were well placed to stop this movement of troops. The Sea King's radar highlighted ground movement to a Canadian MPA in which the CAOC had placed a Joint Terminal Air Attack Controller (JTAC) to cue in the AH. Unlike the previous night the Canadian aircraft had a good picture of the ground and could track multiple technical and main battle tanks on the move. However, it was impossible to determine whether these were PGF reinforcements or advancing FLF units. With this lack of clarity, the Apaches were stood down.

Throughout Sunday it was difficult to take your eyes off of the Sky TV reports as reporter Alex Crawford accompanied the rebels on their apparently unopposed drive into Tripoli. One report included the line that the roads had been cleared during the night by attack helicopter – we hadn't actually flown and I took this as an indicator of how AH had played in the minds of the FLF and Gaddafi forces. The scenes of convoys of rebel vehicles being joined by cheering crowds in the streets were simply amazing. Onboard *OCEAN* we hosted a visit by staff from the French Helicopter Strike Group – a valuable opportunity to compare notes and share operational experiences and lessons so far. Noting the chaos on the ground and the inability to positively identify friend from foe all NATO strike activity was cancelled – including our planned strike for the evening.

Despite the euphoria of the press coverage on the fall off Tripoli it was clear on Monday morning that the fighting was far from over. The regime was holding on to parts of Tripoli and had strongholds in Brega, Sirte and Sabah in the south; eastern Tripoli, Gharyan and Zuwara were still receiving indirect fire from Gaddafi forces. We also received reports of a potential build-up of PGF forces at Bani Walid, some 50nm south-east of Tripoli. General Bouchard gave direction that all deliberate NATO strikes were on hold and that the striking of dynamic targeting would need three-star clearance – reflecting both the confusion on the ground and the wish to avoid striking the FLF or civilians in error.

I was able to update the Fleet Command Group on the latest developments. In the maritime domain a real highlight had been the successful use of Sea King ASAC to cross-cue the Canadian MPA and its camera capability to identify potential AH targets. Despite the lack of UAVs we had found a way to strike coastal targets – if the fluidity of the situation allowed. Looking slightly ahead I also suggested that Fleet might want to start thinking about how to exploit the RFTG's and RN's contribution to the Libya campaign once we were released from CJO's command and media ban. How the operation might end was very much on my mind on Tuesday when we produced a note on the possible extraction of the Task Group. AH tasking was becoming increasingly unlikely and Apaches were needed in Afghanistan so it seemed to me that a 30 September withdrawal was entirely possible. The Apaches spent the evening of 23 August on deck alert but, as was becoming the norm, we were passed no targets.

Wednesday 24 August was an interesting day which demonstrated the strength of our relationship with the French TG. Rear Admiral Coindreau was handing over to Rear Admiral Jean-Baptise Dupuis and I was invited to the French flagship *MISTRAL* to have talks with both commanders. We shared operational lessons and Admiral Coindreau's priorities and thinking were very much aligned with my own, centred on the risk/reward balance of ongoing AH operations and the possible ending of AH strikes. The French with less capable Gazelle helicopters felt, quite rightly, that they were now taking increasing risk for diminishing return − the psychological impact on both PGF and the Gaddafi regime had largely been made. For them the forthcoming handover of helicopter carriers in mid-September when *TONNERRE* would replace *MISTRAL* would be a good point to cease AH operations. Unlike me, they did have real frustration with the CAOC (and I suspect the entire NATO command and control structure). This may have been in part because of their investment in a Helicopter Strike Group Staff in *MISTRAL* rather than an AH cell, like the UK's, in the CAOC. They were still clear that they would continue to conduct national operations and strikes as ordered by Paris regardless of any NATO instructions. We agreed that the campaign had demonstrated the interoperability of the UK and French Task Groups and to maintain the momentum in the spring. The French priority was to develop their amphibious capability and to assist we would embark some of Admiral Philippe's staff into the UK Amphibious flagship for forthcoming exercises. In return they would assist my own preparations for the UK's new carriers entering service by hosting my air planning staff in the French carrier *CHARLES DE GAULLE*'s spring work-up. I was sad to say goodbye to Admiral Philippe − he had been a brother in arms and a first-class ally. We had worked seamlessly and demonstrated what Anglo-French Task Groups could achieve together when our national objectives were completely aligned.

At Thursday's COMOPS 'O group' video conference I reported the outcome of my discussions with my French opposite numbers and updated Admiral Corder on the latest situation on the ground. At this stage we expected to be tasked to the east of Tripoli and further south against Gaddafi's strongholds in Sirte and Sabah. Like the French I felt that the rapid advance of the FLF together with the lack of persistent surveillance resulted in an increasingly confused picture in which allocating AH targets would be increasingly difficult. When considered alongside the need to increase AH numbers in Afghanistan I recommended that Fleet start thinking about when we should cease strikes. Again no targets were found for AHs and it became a no-strike night.

On Friday *OCEAN* was beginning to show the strains of prolonged operations. The ship had in effect been running since the beginning of the year as it prepared for, and then got through, work-up and then deployed. Captain Betton had been calling for a maintenance period since July and one was scheduled for the first two weeks of September but the wear was showing through. On 26 August the ship's electrical generating plants were a worry and of the four diesel generators carried one was unserviceable, one was in need of refurbishment, and one was in poor condition. This was not a sensible basis on which to launch strikes so flying was cancelled and the ship anchored to allow *OCEAN*'s engineers to work on the plants. A quieter evening resulted, and I was asked to visit the flag captain in the helicopter carriers' island mess where I discovered a major breach of security. Somebody had let Captain Andrew know that it was my birthday, and he took the opportunity of being at anchor to host a surprise dinner party for me – complete with homemade balloons and cake. It was a great evening and a welcome chance both to relax and to reflect on how well *OCEAN* had transformed itself into a flagship in which the ship and staff clearly worked well together. Captain Andrew was joined by my policy advisor David Bruce and those from the ship with whom I worked closely: Lieutenant Colonel Lenny Brown, Lieutenant Commanders Ben Keith, Simon Collins and Jim Corbett. I thoroughly enjoyed the evening and was touched by the kindness of the *OCEAN* team.

The weekend was relatively quiet as *OCEAN* slowly headed towards Malta and its maintenance period. For me the focus was increasingly the actions needed to draw the operation to a close and this centred around a report of proceedings (or lessons identified) and nominations for honours and awards for those in the group – including HMS *LIVERPOOL*. The entire staff were involved in producing a comprehensive set of lessons and a much smaller group considered who we would nominate for honours and awards.

Working with Gary Waterfall, I prepared a plan that would see the AH teams return to *OCEAN* for a final two weeks of standing by for operations from mid-September before departing for the UK on 30 September. On the ground, Tripoli was now firmly in FLF hands and fighting was centred around Sirte and Bani Walid. The French, less constrained by the NATO targeting restrictions, did complete a successful AH strike against PGF vehicles around Sirte.

Monday 29 August was *OCEAN*'s last day at sea before its maintenance period and the last Fleet Command Group for a while. I was able to brief Fleet on the difficulties of conducting AH strikes ashore. The CAOC's clear, and correct, priority was to avoid engaging civilians or FLF and as a result if there was any doubt whatsoever about the location of FLF or civilians, strikes were not authorised. I explained that this constraint was not shared by the French HSG whose strikes were increasingly unilateral – but nonetheless, so far, effective. We also received increasing reports of members of Gaddafi's family fleeing to Algeria – one of our indicators of success.

For the next two weeks *OCEAN* underwent much-needed maintenance and many of our people took the opportunity either to spend a few days at home in the UK or to fly their families out to the Mediterranean. In Libya the FLF consolidated their recent gains and the interim government, the National Transitional Council (NTC), moved from Benghazi to Tripoli and on 27 August had been recognised by the Arab League as the legitimate holder of Libya's League seat. The fighting was not, however, done and on 1 September Gaddafi broadcast via a Syrian outlet, refusing to surrender and calling for a guerrilla war against the new government. There was still very much a possibility that some form of stalemate might return. The FLF were still trying to force Sirte and Bani Walid out of PGF hands and, since the fall of Tripoli, were searching for Gaddafi himself.

The end of August also saw the end of Ramadan and General Bouchard ordered an increase in non-lethal pressure on the regime. NATO ships continued broadcasting the NATO message to the PLF encouraging them to lay down their arms and abandon the regime. Overnight on 31 August NATO ships were very active off Sirte – *LIVERPOOL* firing star shells to harass PGF forces. But for the next fortnight there was relatively little movement on the ground with tentative FLF advances towards Bani Walid and Sirte being repelled by Gaddafi forces. By the time I returned to *OCEAN* on 15 September the biggest progress appeared to be political. On 12 September China was the last major power to recognise the NTC and on the 15th itself David Cameron and Sarkozy visited Benghazi and the United Nations passed UNSCR 2009 which extended the no-fly zone and the legal basis for continuing NATO air operations. *OCEAN* was back at sea on Friday 16 September and we were hosting a visit by the Second Sea Lord Vice Admiral Charles Montgomery – who was impressed by the team spirit shown by everyone in *OCEAN* irrespective of service. In Libya the regime was effectively hemmed into Sirte and Bani Walid and even here the front lines were contested – further AH strikes seemed increasingly unlikely. I was also briefed on a developing situation in Somalia where a British citizen had been kidnapped and the fact that options were being developed to provide rescue options that might include *OCEAN*.

On Monday 19 September *OCEAN* was preparing to recommence AH strikes from Wednesday. Internal fuel tanks were fitted into the Apaches to increase their range and enable them to strike in the vicinity of Bani Walid, and the aircrew and CAOC were exploring ingress and exit routes to the area. I had had a very revealing conversation with Admiral Dupuis on the Sunday when he confirmed that he had cancelled his planned strikes for Tuesday and Thursday. Due to the vulnerability of his attack helicopters he ruled out operating further inland than Sirte and felt that AH operations were now at an end. So that he was seen to be in step with the Brits he wanted to know what the UK plans were for withdrawal. Like the very first strike in

June this the ending of AH operations was becoming a very much a political and presentational issue.

The weekly Fleet Command Group was delayed to Tuesday when I was able to report the mood music and the approaching end of AH operations – as confirmed by the situation on the ground, Admiral Dupius and General Joddice – since after all most of the Libyan population were now safe from PGF fire. My advice was that we should seek the earliest presentationally acceptable point to withdraw. The rest of the week saw an increasing sense that AH operations would imminently finish and a growing chance that *OCEAN* would be sent east of Suez to provide a big deck for the potential hostage rescue.

On Thursday I spoke to Admiral Harding in Naples who confirmed that for NATO AH operations were over. On the ground the FLF seized the Al-Jufrah oasis leaving the PGF in control of only Sirte and Ban Walid. In another twist I received a call from the Navy's personnel department to say that my two-year tour as COMUKTG would come to an end after only 11 months in November. My credentials as a Task Group Commander could not be any stronger and I was to be the Head of Naval Resources and Plans – the job Commodore Tim Laurence had done all those years ago. I received the news with mixed emotions – I had hoped to be Head of Navy RP one day but there was still a great done to be done as COMUKTG. The role of COMUKTG and the RFTG remained new concepts that needed championing within the Navy and Defence.

The rumours continued about the formal end of AH operations and the emerging tasking for *OCEAN* off Somalia – confirmed on Saturday 24 September when NATO approved the ship's departure and the prime minister directed *OCEAN* east. This left me to have my final phone call (of hundreds) with the ever-supportive Paul Abraham and for the staff and me to disembark on 25 September. After 170 days the maritime strike mission was complete.

Throughout early October the FLF slowly gained ground around Sirte and by the 13th the PGF were clinging onto the western third of the city. Four days later Bani Walid fell into FLF hands. On 20 October the remaining PGF in Sirte decided that their positions were untenable and attempted to break out of the city in a convoy of vehicles. Having fought its way out of the city the convoy was eventually stopped by a combination of air strikes and FLF fighters. In the resulting chaos Gaddafi, his son Mutassim and ex-defence minister Abu Bakr Yuniis were killed. Three days later the NTC announced the liberation of Libya and NATO operations effectively ceased on 31 October.

CHAPTER SEVEN

Lessons

As we entered the last few weeks in the Mediterranean the staff and I spent a great deal of time compiling and assessing what we had learned from our experiences – and the very first launching of maritime strike from the new Response Force Task Group (RFTG). At the outset it was hard not to be impressed by how quickly the RFTG had gone into action after being established in February. What is more, of the various potential tasks that we might have been expected to undertake, launching Apache strikes was perhaps one of the more unexpected. And what had been planned as a routine exercise deployment designed to test the new RFTG concept and its staff became a full-blown operational deployment.

The first key take-away was that the new Task Group construct worked. Combining the previous Amphibious and Carrier Strike staffs into a single team produced a battle staff able to deliver the full range of potential tasks. Similarly, the Task Group itself with its combination of amphibious and aviation assets offered maximum flexibility, being able to rapidly re-role to deliver whatever was asked of it. Throughout *Cougar* this flexibility of capability and thinking was reflected in the wide range of potential tasks that the staff planned and the options we offered to London. Before committing to Apache strikes the TG had planned three non-combatant evacuation operations, the interdiction of inshore Libyan coast traffic, the delivery and protection of humanitarian stores into Misrata, options to place psychological pressure on the Gaddafi regime and amphibious assault.

Key to this flexibility was the preparation conducted before deploying, to prepare the individual units and staff. The fact that

ALBION, LIVERPOOL, SUTHERLAND and *MOUNTS BAY* had operated together almost constantly for the previous 18 months created a valuable understanding between them. Similarly *ALBION* was a well worked-up and capable flagship – designed to support two large staffs – and its captain, James Morley, was a practised and highly effective flag captain who ensured that his senior team integrated seamlessly with the staff. The fact that the new COMUKTG staff had been largely formed out of the Amphibious staff who had deployed in the ship the previous year aided this process. Exercise *Green Alligator*, held on *ALBION* in Devonport before *Cougar*, enabled us to give the new COMUKTG and elements of 3 Cdo Bde team an invaluable first run out.

So when we deployed I was supported by a well-found and trained battle staff in a purpose-built command ship which was at the heart of the Group's capability. This was a stark contrast to what I had experienced in the past where battle staffs were often made up of augmentees with little specific training or experience working together in a jury-rigged headquarters. The other key development was the addition of a properly constructed Operational Intelligence Support Cell which ensured that the staff had enhanced situational awareness and excellent intelligence support. As a result, from day one of the deployment the battle staff were able to be on the front foot and throughout the deployment were able to develop contingency plans and options for the government.

Very quickly the deployment highlighted the need to think differently about contingency. To my mind *Cougar* proved the value of deploying a balanced Task Group with a baseline of capability and training into a region where its capability might be needed. Once deployed the Group could simultaneously enhance its capability while developing and offering potential options for tasking. This capability baseline was provided by the excellent training delivered by Flag Officer Sea Training in the UK – who continued to provide support to the group in the Mediterranean. Once deployed a flexibility of mind is needed by all in the Task Group – and not just the staff – that meant that we had to accept and indeed embrace levels of uncertainty that naval personnel were simply not used to. Deploying to offer choice means not having a fixed programme to which ships strictly adhere – and if required not even fixed deployment dates. This was a first for most of us in the Group and required real leadership from Task Group commanding officers to ensure that their people remained focused and motivated throughout. Logistical support of the group is a key issue to which I will return. This was initially compounded by the fact that we sailed in April without dedicated support and the diplomatic clearance for international port visits. In the opening weeks of the deployment we were therefore very fortunate to be able to call upon Gibraltar and the Sovereign Base Areas in Cyprus for support and in Cyprus' case to enable our amphibious and later attack helicopter training.

The deployment depended on its support ships to maintain its capability and sustain subsequent operations. During the AH strike period the stores ship *FORT ROSALIE* provided essential support with its regular resupplies of essential equipment, stores and on occasion aircraft. It also had essential amphibious and munitions embarked and was a key enabler of the entire range of our potential group operations. With a wide range of NATO and national naval units off the Libyan coast there was also a pressing need for oilers to sustain the coalition effort. *OCEAN* benefitted from a fuel-efficient machinery plant, but UK tankers (*ORANGELEAF* and *WAVE KNIGHT*) made a significant contribution to the wider maritime effort. Apart from the reduction of risk to aircrew I probably spent most of my time considering logistics related issues revolving around how we might sustain the Task Group. This ranged from stores and support to medical and personnel issues.

The risk to aircrew quickly brought the related issues of joint personnel recovery and medical support into sharp focus. The gap in UK military capability to recover downed aircrew from hostile or contested battlespace was a real concern – only really dealt with by the embarkation of the USAF HH-60G Pave Hawk helicopters and the teams from the USAF 56th Rescue Squadron. The medical challenge was more fundamental. By 2011 the UK military were used to campaigning in Afghanistan and Iraq where good casualty pathways were in place, supported in Afghanistan by airborne Medical Emergency Response Teams. Off Libya, and indeed in most future contingent operations, this level of support cannot be provided but once again we were able to improve the medical support by embarking a surgical team in *OCEAN*. A further concern was the absence of a helicopter able to hover, and therefore winch, at night, meaning that we were unable to recover downed aircrew from the sea when we might need to.

The operation proved the flexibility of large flat-decked ships like *OCEAN*. It had quickly adapted into a flagship and although it could not have hosted a full COMUKTG staff it was able to support the smaller maritime strike team that I took with me. *OCEAN* could not offer the same planning spaces, flag operations room, accommodation or communications ability as *ALBION* but it did all that was needed for maritime strike – and did it well. *OCEAN* was also able to seamlessly re-role from amphibious assault to maritime strike by rapidly changing its tailored air group. The Sea King HC4 troop carriers were effectively replaced by increased numbers of Apache, Sea King ASAC and HH-60 Pave Hawks. It also had the space onboard to accommodate not only my small staff but also the surgical team.

The deployment also highlighted the complexities of operating a national Task Group in support of a NATO campaign. The fact that it worked so well was due in no small part to the UK Maritime Component Commander in Northwood (Rear Admiral Ian Corder) and the placement of two other British admirals in key NATO posts – Rear Admiral Russ Harding as the NATO Deputy Joint Commander and Jon Westbrook as the Deputy NATO Maritime Component Commander. I was pleasantly surprised by the lack of interference from above and could not have been better supported by these three. In particular Admiral Ian – and Captain Paul Abraham often on his behalf – provided substantial top cover and the conduit between COMUKTG and both the Fleet and PJHQ staff, protecting me, and more importantly my very small team in *OCEAN*, from countless questions and bureaucracy that would have otherwise arisen. The relationship between the UK and NATO was not as smooth as it perhaps could have been. I was surprised by how many UK video conferences I attended at which NATO was not mentioned at all, despite the UK effort being a relatively small – albeit important – part of a wider NATO campaign. The fact that in 2011 the UK filled a number of key NATO posts in the Naples headquarters helped bridge this gap and played an important part in making this relationship work.

For me, apart from the NATO headquarters and Northwood the key operational relationships were with the French Task Group Commander Rear Admiral Coindreau and the Italian (NATO) Task Group Commander Admiral Foffi. The French Task Group was impressive both in terms of approach and capability – and with its fixed-wing carrier gave us a glimpse of the future Royal Navy with the Queen Elizabeth-class carriers. In terms of operations off Libya the RN and French Task and associated Helicopter Strike Groups worked hand in hand. They also stood out as the only navies involved – the USN having not taken part – able to project power ashore. In the RN's case by TLAM, Apaches and amphibious forces and the French by carrier strike and amphibious forces. Importantly they could both command these operations from the sea with well-formed and trained battle staffs and properly equipped command platforms, and sustain those operations for prolonged periods. Both shared a similar view of operations and were clearly trained and prepared for high-intensity conflict, therefore could plan and if needed execute the full range of naval operations.

The Italian Task Group meanwhile was more constrained by commanding a range of coalition units and the staff had for some time been focused on NATO Operation *Active Endeavour* – the operation to prevent the movement of terrorists or weapons of mass destruction in the Mediterranean. This involved building a recognised maritime picture and challenging and, if necessary, inspecting transiting merchant vessels. These are important maritime security and policing operations and having focused on this level of operations it was difficult to shift to warfighting. They were however excellent at scheduling NATO warships off and onto station. The takeaway being that it is better to train your ships and battle staffs for the higher-intensity operations since this will enable them to carry out every type of operation – including the less demanding ones. Conversely, to focus, prepare and in some cases equip for less demanding roles provides forces not capable of high-intensity operations.

In terms of the units that took part in the campaign Libya reaffirmed the need for a balance of capabilities. I have already covered the essential role of the command platform, battle staffs and Royal Fleet Auxiliaries (tankers and stores ships). Submarines also played a key role. As a precursor to the air campaign UK submarines conducted precision Tomahawk strikes that neutralised Libyan air defences. Thereafter UK, French and other NATO submarines provided important intelligence and conducted surveillance operations, often operating close inshore.

French and British amphibious forces also played their role – the presence of both *ALBION* and *OCEAN* off Brega in June played an important part in convincing the Gaddafi regime that some form of amphibious assault was likely and inspired the subsequent diversion of regime resources to construct beach defences. The amphibious elements of the Task Group were key elements of the majority of the tasks we were asked to plan prior to the launching of Apache strikes. Amphibious forces were earmarked to deliver and protect humanitarian aid in Misrata, to conduct a number of non-combatant evacuation operations and to interdict Libyan coastal traffic.

The destroyers and frigates that operated off Libya carried out a number of roles including surveillance, intelligence gathering and naval fires. They also played an important role in reassuring the coastal civilian population by their presence and the use of radio in a box to transmit supportive messages, and similarly unsettled PGF forces by the same means and in *LIVERPOOL*'s case the use of star shell. There has been a debate in naval circles for some years by those who argued that destroyers and frigates should not be called escorts, since this term undervalued the flexibility and capability of these highly complex warships. Yet, as a commander having to place a large, fairly vulnerable, helicopter carrier close to a hostile shore every evening I was very aware of their value in the traditional escort role. Certainly, once the Libyan anti-ship missiles were unaccounted for the presence of a destroyer or frigate between the coast and *OCEAN* was essential. The final naval capability that played a significant role was mine countermeasures. Both *BROCKLESBY* and *BANGOR* operated close to the Libyan shore conducting operations to ensure Misrata was kept clear of mines which Gaddafi forces were known to have laid. Although operating under the NATO shield in the flagship we were kept informed of their progress, activities and positions and stood by to provide assistance if needed.

Once the Task Group commenced maritime strike operations the focus became aviation. What the Apache crews and support staff achieved was truly remarkable and underscored the capability of the Apache to operate in the most challenging circumstances – including facing the latest generation of man-portable anti-air missiles. We planned 47 missions but only flew 22, the others being cancelled largely due to the lack of persistent surveillance or the inability to identify valid targets. That said, the 22 completed missions achieved a great deal – not only in kinetic terms (54 technicals, two RHIBS, four main battle tanks, four MANPADS, three command and control nodes, three anti-aircraft guns, two BM-21 rocket launchers and one ZSU mounted anti-aircraft gun) but more importantly psychologically. Rob Weighill and Florence Gaub wrote in their book on NATO's campaign in Libya: 'Helicopter raids in Brega and Az-Zawiyah were cited specifically as examples where the destructive physical effects on the regime forces had undermined their cohesion and morale significantly.'[1]

The operation proved the utility of AHs being launched from the sea, maximising the helicopter carriers' ability to reposition and launch strikes where they are least expected. The use of two Apaches on 12 June to strike the PGF Special Forces RHIBS also demonstrated their ability to operate against maritime targets. In addition we demonstrated the ability of Royal Navy Sea Kings to co-ordinate strikes and utilise their radar's ability to detect moving targets ashore to vector Apaches, UAVs and MPAs onto target – both on the aground and on the sea. And a bit like the escort case, the anti-ship missile threat reminded us all of the Sea Kings' vital role providing force protection to the Task Group and *OCEAN*.

So for me the main capability lesson for the future is to deploy Task Groups with the full range of capabilities that are able to seamlessly re-role from amphibious to strike operations – and everything in between. This is the way to ensure that we offer the greatest range of military options to the government – what the Armed Forces are for. This also means that an integrated battle staff is needed, able to plan and execute the full range of operations from amphibious to carrier strike.

★★

Command is a deeply human and personal activity and my 170 days deployed as COMUKTG tested me in ways that I had not experienced before. There was the very personal challenge of putting UK servicepeople in harm's way with the expectation of losing some, and the associated feelings surrounding ordering strikes that would inevitably result in deaths amongst the PGF. The only way to deal with the former was to do the most I could to reduce the risks to the aircrew; and with the latter, to be clear in my own mind about the legal and moral basis of what we were doing in Libya. This meant understanding the various UN Security Council Resolutions and being sure that all the unit commanders and aircrew had a thorough understanding of the limitations of the Rules of Engagement and associated target directives. It was nonetheless tiring and demanding work and I had to keep a close eye on ensuring I got enough rest and time away from the job. Hence the importance of some down time and the occasional run around the upper deck.

An important part of the role was building and maintaining relationships with those for whom I worked – and the various stakeholders in the myriad headquarters with which we interfaced. I was lucky in that in my 27 years in the Navy I had come across many with whom I worked – and importantly I enjoyed their trust. This included the Commander and Deputy Commander in Chief Fleet and the numerous admirals with whom I interacted – Duncan Potts, Ian Corder, Russ Harding and Jon Westbrook. The interface with NATO and the Fleet

Headquarters therefore worked well, built on this mutual trust. With hindsight I probably failed to spend enough time getting to know the various staff officers in the Permanent Joint Headquarters. I knew Chief of Staff (Ops) Major General Messenger and of course the Chief of Joint Operations himself, Air Marshal Stuart Peach, but not those in the key posts around him. I suspect that my difficulties around press briefings originated from this staff rather than the Commander himself. In my defence, however, I only had a few weeks in post before deploying and I used my time getting to know the commanders of the Group and the COMUKTG staff – which was probably right.

The personal rapport between Admiral Coindreau and me was a real strength and underpinned unpredicted levels of Anglo-French co-operation. We talked openly to each other, sharing operational lessons as well as our concerns and worries over the risk/reward balance of our respective AH strikes. Put simply, it could not have been better. I also learnt that the selection of the right individuals to be my liaison officers paid real dividends. When presented with a list of liaison posts to be filled there is always a tendency to send some of your less capable people, leaving the very best in the core staff. Libya proved the reverse. Your liaison officer must not only be extremely capable, but he/she must be in your mind and able to intuitively represent your thoughts to the commander and staff they are attached to. All my liaison officers scattered around the Mediterranean – in *CHARLES DE GAULLE*, the *GARIBALDI*, the Maritime Component and the Joint Headquarters and the CAOC – did a first-class and often unseen job.

The integrated COMUKTG and 3 Cdo battle staff with which we sailed provided an impressive planning capability. Looking back I underestimated the number of staff I should have taken across to *OCEAN* with me. I was trying to balance the staff needed to support James Morley in *ALBION* as he headed east and those needed to support me in the maritime strike role. While I got it largely right I probably took too few across with me – and especially in the key logistics area. The result was that during the busy period prior to the September stand-down the staff and I had little spare capacity and were running red hot. The fact it worked reflected the quality of the small team – co-ordinated by the outstanding chief of staff Al Livingstone and the support of Andrew Betton as the flag captain and *OCEAN*'s heads of department. Another important lesson was the value of diversity of thought within the staff. In this the policy advisor David Bruce played a key role and his constructive challenge and often alternative perspective was more than helpful.

When I worked for the Vice Chief of Defence, General Sir Timothy Granville Chapman, when presenting he often used slides which compared the role of the commander and of the staff. I kept his points in mind throughout Libya and they proved true. The commander's role was to:

> **Understand the one- and two-up intent.** In directing the activity of the Task Group and developing potential options for operations it was key that I understood the intent of CINCLEET (and later CJO) and indeed the strategic context in which I operated. This worked well, assisted by David Bruce's direct feed from Whitehall. Importantly this included a thorough understanding of the levels of risk that government was willing to expose UK personnel to. Put another way, keeping the strategic requirements in mind ensures that the commander keeps a broader perspective and is able to prevent the team from the pitfall of focusing on the tactical problem and missing the overall objective of what is trying to be achieved.
>
> **Think the unthinkable.** Keeping the bigger picture in mind also enables the commander to challenge the staff and ask the more difficult questions. From the outset I was very aware of the risks our aircrew would be taking and before the first strike I asked the team to ensure that all the preparations were in place to deal with the loss of an Apache and the handling of both casualties and deaths amongst the Group. Initially the staff may have felt that I was being overly dramatic but after the first few strikes they fully realised that these preparations were needed. Similarly it was me who: focused the team on a possible surface-to-surface missile threat when the missiles went missing

from Libyan warships; questioned how we would rebut any regime claims that we had killed civilians or hit civilian targets; asked if we should protect the identities of those interviewed by the press to protect them from potential retribution; and asked if we had an obligation to recover the casualties from the Apache strike on the SF RHIBs.

Think 'What next?' Very quickly the team became focused on the various battle rhythms within the group. For *OCEAN* the cycle of stand-offs when luminosity prevented strikes and the replenishment cycle with *FORT ROSALIE* became important, as did the careful balance of strike, maintenance and rest days. For the staff and AH teams the Air Tasking Order Cycle became key: within 36 hours targets were developed by the onboard team and the AH cell in the CAOC before appearing in the ATO. This left the Chief of Staff and me to think longer term and consider some of the broader issues. In particular even up to August there appeared to be every chance that Libya would be divided between Gaddafi and the rebels and that his power might endure. Hence my initiating the work to maintain the RFTG off Libya into 2012 – potentially to continue AH strikes or indeed to support post-conflict operations.

Deal with external agencies/media. Looking back I spent a considerable amount of time, and energy, dealing with the various headquarters who had a part in the campaign. I alone dealt with the politics involved and ensured that the staff and those delivering the strikes were, as far as possible, able to focus on their important work without distraction. I was at the forefront of our engagement with the media and wore the resulting fallout – and again kept this from the team.

Give direction/take difficult decisions. There is real danger in complex and challenging circumstances that pressure and stress prevent effective decision making. The balance is between seeking and gaining the maximum views and consensus and the autocratic style of leadership sometimes, incorrectly, associated with military command. In my view there is a comfortable relationship between the two. I genuinely valued everyone's views – and particularly those that highlighted alternative perspectives and analysis of the problem. I would consider these and then come to a view and give direction. The situation never arose in which this direction was challenged but Al Livingstone (chief of staff), James Morley/Andrew Betton (as flag captain), Jason Etherington (with regard to the use of Apache) and David Bruce knew that I would welcome such a challenge if they needed to make one. But they also accepted that while their views were important and would be considered, once I came to a decision they would support it. It is absolutely the commander's role to give direction and take the difficult decisions – and be comfortable with, and accept, the ramifications.

Own the risk. Throughout the deployment my priority was to reduce the risk to all in the Task Group, and when conducting Apache strikes the aircrew, by doing all I could do to both ensure success and consider all the possibilities that might arise. With the Apache strikes the managing of risk was effectively a double act between Gary Waterfall and me. Gary as the national red card holder within the CAOC would veto any task that exceeded the national appetite for risk. The only exception to this was the strike on the SF RHIBS which was carried out under the Maritime Component Commander (Northwood) with the execute order delegated entirely to me. At every Go/ No Go brief I would additionally consider the maritime factors (sea state, weather, the maritime picture threat etc.), the latest intelligence and importantly input from Jason Etherington and the lead aircrew about to launch the mission. I know the aircrew appreciated the opportunity to both hear and take part in the discussion and knew that whatever the CAOC direction, if having heard all the inputs at the brief I was not content, they would not launch. Every time I gave the Go decision I was looking at the lead for the mission. We all knew who was taking the risk – them – and who owned it.

Energise the circuits. Prolonged operations all have their periods of inactivity and monotony. For us this was particularly the case in September when the Apaches were often held at deck readiness but not launched, combined with maintenance and non-strike days. Routine becomes everything and there is a real danger of lethargy resulting in the loss of focus and the thinking edge so important for the battle staff. I was very aware that I was under the greatest personal stress of the staff and at times the most tired – in addition to the daily strike and staff routines I was attending video conferences to higher headquarters and liaising with external agencies and other commanders. In addition, I was in the operations room throughout every overnight strike. It was key therefore that I became aware of the danger of being overtired and setting the wrong tone. I needed to approach every meeting/briefing with the same enthusiasm and energy that I did at the first and my direction, guidance and presence had to energise all in the Group. This was mirrored by Andy Betton and the squadron commanding officers in *OCEAN*. Energizing the circuits is a key, and often overlooked, command function.

Using the same format the staff's key roles can be summarised as:

Identify/consider the factors. The staff take the commander's interpretation of the strategic direction and his or her own direction and guidance and identify and explore the various factors that could shape or influence events. From this they provide and develop potential courses of action which together with the commander they consider before presenting them for selection.

Know the detail and be subject matter experts. Individual staff officers were selected because of their expertise in their various specialisations. It is important that the commander acknowledges where this expertise lies and accepts that they are not the tactical know-all that their rank or position might suggest. For example, when I embarked in *ALBION* it was only six months since I had been the ship's captain. However, even after such a short period of time I was out of date and did not have the capacity, or the need, to concern myself with the tactical issues in the ship – this was rightly the concern of James Morley. Similarly, my Principal Warfare Officers Course, good as it was, was 16 years before I became COMUKTG. In terms of tactical detail, I therefore relied on my warfare lieutenant commanders' advice. There is a tendency for us all to return to comfort zones and, if we are not careful, tactical detail, but this is certainly not appropriate when leading a battle staff and will make the team's task more difficult and take up the commander's capacity that should be used elsewhere.

Translate commander's intent into action. On a similar theme it is the staff's role to take the commander's intent and make it happen. As COMUKTG the most obvious example of this was the daily intentions signal that gave orders to the Task Group for the following 24 hours. This would be discussed at the morning command brief and my direction and guidance formally given at the evening command brief. The chief of staff would, with staff input, translate this into a draft signal that would be cleared by the flag captain before being brought to me for release at approx. 2100 every evening. Once issued the flag captain would ensure that in the next 24 hours all the ships and units in the group were in the right position at the right time to deliver the required effect.

Tell the commander what is not possible! To me this is the most important role of the staff. It is very easy in a hierarchical military structure in which the majority have come through similar career paths for group think and an unhealthy deference to rank to exist. Military personnel are by nature positive and can-do – but this must be balanced by realism and a thorough understanding of the risks of any proposed course of action. Very importantly, for every potential option that we generated throughout the deployment I included an assessment of what we could not do, associated risks of what we might do and a list of additional support we might require. This sort of assessment is only possible if the staff are indeed telling the commander what is not possible.

For me the most challenging period of the deployment – when we launched our first Apache strikes and transferred from *ALBION* to *OCEAN* – was made much more difficult by the misunderstanding over our media engagement – and my sacking. As I have explained the fallout of the Strategic Defence and Security Review and the distrust between the Royal Navy and Royal Air Force played its part in this. The fact that I had followed my media handler and MOD drafted lines to take gave me the confidence to press on with the job. Unfortunately, one result of the spat was effectively a media ban on anything from the group which meant that the contribution of the RN (and Army Air Corps) did not get the reporting it deserved – which was keenly felt by the sailors, Marines and soldiers involved. I could only reassure them that their efforts were known in the Ministry of Defence and their parent services.

There was a danger that any reporting, including of the lessons, would be seized upon in ongoing RN/RAF disputes. With the carrier strike programme still underway both services were looking at how strike operations might be commanded. For me a major lesson of maritime strike off Libya was that in command and control terms *Ellamy* was a model for the future – but not necessarily *the* model. Off Libya the CAOC and Air Component Commander sat ashore and commanded the air campaign – which worked well. An alternative model could see the CAOC sitting afloat in a suitable command platform and for smaller amphibious operation the airspace above the designated amphibious operating area could be commanded by the Amphibious Commander. My advice was that this was not an either/

or decision, and that Defence should be open to all these approaches – selecting the most appropriate command and control architecture for the situation.

The other area where single services' agendas raised their heads was sadly recognition for the remarkable bravery of the Apache aircrew. As our part in the Libya campaign came to a close I held an honours and awards committee to decide who we would nominate for national awards. When considering the guidelines for such awards the Apache aircrew stood out. They had flown 22 missions at extremely low altitude, facing (and being engaged by) the most advanced shoulder-launched anti-aircraft missiles and gunfire. Their bravery was obvious. I forwarded my nominations to the Maritime Component Commander and achieved some success – but not all the Apache pilots received the recognition they deserved.

My formal lessons paper was submitted and went up the command and on my return to the UK I conducted office calls on the Commander and Deputy Commander in Chief Fleet. Both thanked me for a job well done and Vice Admiral Zambellas highlighted how well I had handled the fallout of the media interviews. He was aware of the difficulties I found myself in and was standing by to intervene but felt that he didn't need to because of the way I played down the spat and got on with the job. I back-briefed Fleet and FOST staff on the operation and later went with Air Commodore Ed Stringer (the first UKACC in Naples) to Australia and New Zealand to brief them on what we had learned – as we had been off Libya, we were a good double act. For me the most revealing call was on the Chief of Defence Staff, General Sir David Richards, who I saw in his office in London. I talked him through the operation and said that in my view the Libya and the RFTG had been Defence at its best – Army and Royal Navy helicopters operating from Royal Navy platforms in support of an air campaign. I also highlighted how well the Army (and USAF) teams had fitted into *OCEAN* and of course how brave the Army aircrew had been. He thanked me for a job well done and as I left the room asked if there was any truth in the rumours that he had heard that the RAF had blocked media from Task Group. I replied that while

I couldn't say that, there was a clear disconnect between the media lines given by the MOD and PJHQ. Yes, he said, he knew all about it and thanked me again. As if this was not good enough I bumped into the Chief of the General Staff, General Sir Peter Wall, in the corridor – he too thanked me for a job well done and for looking after the Army people in the Task Group so well.

We had achieved remarkable things, and before committing to maritime strike had offered a range of options to HM government including non-combatant evacuation operations in Syria, Yemen and Libya and amphibious options for Libya and interdiction operations off the coast. And then we had, for the first time ever, used Army attack helicopters to launch and sustain maritime strike from HMS *OCEAN*. For me the measures of success were achieved – we had offered options, placed psychological pressure on the Gaddafi regime and done our part to protect the civilian population of Libya. Most importantly to me we had achieved all this and lost no one.

The best summary of what the Navy had achieved was in the First Sea Lord's signal of 31 October issued on the formal ending of operations off Libya:

PERSONAL FROM FIRST SEA LORD, ADMIRAL SIR MARK STANHOPE GCB OBE ADC: END OF OP ELLAMY/OP UNIFIED PROTECTOR.

AS OPERATIONS OFF LIBYA DRAW TO A CLOSE, I WANTED TO CONGRATULATE YOU ALL ON THE EXCEPTIONAL CONTRIBUTION MADE BY NAVAL FORCES THROUGHOUT THIS CAMPAIGN.

FOR OVER EIGHT MONTHS THE ROYAL NAVY AND ROYAL FLEET AUXILIARY HAVE BEEN DEPLOYED ON ACTIVE SERVICE IN SUPPORT OF THE LIBYAN PEOPLE UNDER BOTH NATIONAL AND NATO COMMAND. THE OPERATIONAL EFFECT ACHIEVED BY OUR MARITIME FORCES HAS BEEN SIGNIFICANT AND, WORKING ALONGSIDE OUR SISTER SERVICES AND COALITION PARTNERS, YOU HAVE ONCE AGAIN DEMONSTRATED THE FLEXIBILITY, AGILITY AND FIGHTING POWER THAT ARE THE TRADE MARKS OF THE FLEET.

YOU HAVE BEEN INVOLVED IN A HUGE RANGE OF ACTIVITY INCLUDING EVACUATING CIVILIANS, PRECISION TLAM STRIKE, SUPPORTING AND DELIVERING AH OPERATIONS, VITAL MINE CLEARNACE AND ROUTE SURVEYS TO ENSURE THE FREEDOM OF THE LIBYAN COASTAL WATERS AND DELIVERY OF HUMANITARIAN

AID, CO-ORDINATED NAVAL FIRES SUPPORT AND EMBARGO AND MARITIME SECURITY OPERATIONS, ALL UNDERWRITTEN BY THE UNFAILING LOGISTIC SUPPORT OF THE RFA. IN EACH OF THESE AREAS YOU HAVE EXCELLED AND, AS I AM, YOU SHOULD BE VERY PROUD OF WHAT YOU HAVE ACHIEVED

AT A TIME WHEN OUR FORCES WERE ALREADY HEAVILY EMPLOYED AROUND THE WORLD ON A NUMBER OF STANDING TASKS, AND WHILE THE ROYAL MARINES HAD THE LEAD IN HERRICK, TO BE ABLE TO GENERATE AND SUSTAIN 17 PLATFORMS, WITH OVER 3100 PEOPLE INCLUDING SHIPS' COMPANIES, EMBARKED FORCES AND AIRCREWS, IS A REMARKABLE ACHIEVEMENT AND A TESTAMENT TO YOUR DEDICATION, INNOVATION AND DETEMINATION. I HAVE AGAIN BEEN STRUCK BY THE VALUE OF OUR NAVAL ETHOS AND SPIRIT, BOTH IN THE FRONT LINE AND IN SUPPORT ORGANISATIONS, IN DELIVERING OPERATIONAL SUCCESS.

OUR TASK NOW IS TO REFOCUS ON OUR IMPORTANT STANDING COMMITMENTS AROUND THE WORLD AND TO RESET OUR CONTINGENT CAPABILITY. PROGRAMMES WILL BE ADJUSTED AND RESHAPED TO SHIFT THE FLEET'S FOCUS AND REBALANCE OUR FORCES. WHILE THIS MAY BRING SOME SHORT-TERM UNCERTAINTY, ESPECIALLY FOR UNITS DIRECTLY INVOLVED OR EARMARKED, I INTEND THIS WILL BE KEPT TO A MINIMUM. FUTURE TASKING WILL REFLECT OUR COLLECTIVE PRIORITY TO BE A WORLD CLASS NAVY, READY TO FIGHT AND WIN, AND I LOOK FORWARD TO YOUR CONTINUED SUPPORT AS WE LOOK TOWARDS 2012.

THE NAVAL SERVICE'S CONTRIBUTION IN THE MEDITERRANEAN HAS BEEN OUTSTANDING. I THANK YOU FOR YOUR COURAGE AND ADAPTABILITY AND FOR DELIVERING THE MARITIME COMPONENT OF OUR ARMED FORCES SO RESOLUTELY AND PROFESSIONALLY

BZ

CHAPTER EIGHT

What Came Next

My last few weeks as COMUKTG were busy. In October I embarked in the assault ship HMS *BULWARK* as it completed its regeneration from upkeep to replace HMS *ALBION* as the amphibious and fleet flagship. The ship was off Stornoway in north-east Scotland with some of my staff embarked taking part in a regular large NATO exercise known as *Joint Warrior*. It was very evident that Captain Alex Burton and his ship were ready in all respects to take the duty and gained my validation. A week later I flew my broad pennant at sea for the last time when I joined HMS *ILLUSTRIOUS*, now re-roled as a helicopter carrier, as it prepared to replace HMS *OCEAN* enabling the Mighty 'O' to enter a much-needed refit. The big ships and their commander were handing over. On 15 November I handed over command of the Response Force Task Group to Commodore Paddy McAlpine and a week later I was the Head of Naval Resources and Plans.

I was more than a little sad to leave the Task Group so early since it was important that the lessons of the last six months were fully embraced and the new RFTG/COMUKTG construct firmly established. That said, in 2011 the First Sea Lord, Admiral Sir Mark Stanhope, carefully considered which senior officer went where and he clearly felt that the combination of my newly won operational and established Head Office credibility would enable to me to fight the Navy's case in Whitehall.

The Head of Naval RP had to serve two masters. My boss in terms of reporting and accountability was Major General Mark Poffley (Assistant Chief of the Defence Staff (Resources and Plans)) who reported to Air Marshal Steve Hillier (Deputy Chief of the Defence

Staff (Capability)). My role was effectively to act as the maritime advisor to them and the MOD's finance director – the impressive civil servant David Williams. This required me to understand the various outputs required of the Navy and ensure that they were being cost-effectively delivered. My other boss was the First Sea Lord, Admiral Sir Mark Stanhope, to whom I provided advice on the Central MOD's financial position and shared my analysis of how Defence and his own budgetary area were performing. The trick was to keep the Centre informed of what the Navy was delivering and where efficiencies could be made and the Navy making the best case for the resources it needed. Fundamentally, I was a Centre officer and was greatly aided by the fact that the Navy was largely both cost-efficient in delivering its outputs and its future spending priorities sat comfortably within Defence priorities.

With SDSR 2010 so recently announced and implementation underway you might have expected the defence budget to have been balanced and facing no great pressures at the time. Sadly, this was not the case and the future equipment programme remained unaffordable and was placing huge pressure on the defence budget. At the same time the reorganisation of Defence following SDSR would see responsibility and funding of the future equipment programmes being transferred from the Head Office to the front-line commands. In such circumstances single service agendas were once again very alive and the service staffs argued for their share of resources to be delegated and for their programmes to survive – when not all could.

A major part of resolving this and indeed of the annual budget cycle was my working with the other Heads of RP to create spending and savings packages that balanced the single-service environmental needs with the available resources and defence priorities – a process known as basket weaving. Key to this was the excellent working relationship that I enjoyed with my fellow one-star heads of resources/plans, Brigadier Alistair Dickinson (Army RP), Air Commodore Richard Knighton (Air RP) and Brigadier John Patterson (Joint RP). With us single-service agendas and emotion simply would not win – it was all about what was right for defence priorities and outputs.

The DNRP team were therefore required to really understand how the naval programme was constructed and how every aspect of it contributed to Defence outputs. Together with the other RP divisions we would spot duplication, best practice and inefficiency. My civilian deputy was the ever-present Mike Davis who had been my boss when I worked in DNRP seven years earlier and Captain Navy Plans was Captain Steve Dainton – who I had last met when he was driving *CUMBERLAND* at the start of the *Cougar* deployment. We were supported by eight commander-level desk officers who were subject matter experts for their various areas (surface ships, aviation, manpower, littoral manoeuvre, ISTAR, submarines and plans, the job I had done as Commander). Traditionally DNRP was the training ground for the Navy's future MOD warriors and attracted the very best talent – and 2011 was no exception.

Understanding the programme was one thing but being able to explain and justify individual programmes to the MOD was a key part of the Directorates and indeed my role. During my time the big issues were the future of the amphibious capability, carrier strike, naval personnel numbers and how financial delegation to the front line commands might work – and in most of these areas to one extent or another my Libya experience played in. The amphibious capability and specifically the future of 3 Commando Brigade and the Lead Commando Group that the Brigade generated came sharply into focus as a result of the Army 2020 study that looked to disinvest in the number of soldiers (artillery, engineers and logistics support) supporting the Marines. Every aspect of the Brigade and UK's amphibious capability was rightly challenged.

The post-SDSR structure provided a Brigade Headquarters which would combine with COMUKTG staff to provide the integrated battle staff along the lines of that which deployed with me on *Cougar*. The brigade consisted of three Commando units (40, 42 and 45) which would take their turn combining with Army logistics, engineers, artillery and Commando aviation to form the Lead Commando Group (LCG). The LCG would be held at very high readiness – either in the UK or afloat in amphibious shipping. Each Commando (and its attendant LCG) would hold the duty for six months. The LCG could be up to 1,800 people strong and required considerable support from the Army which some in the Army 2020 team wanted to reduce. However, the LCG provided an extremely versatile and useful force and despite any single-service agenda was a key Defence output within departmental policy papers and the recent review.

In the months that followed the LCG construct and indeed the whole amphibious capability was questioned. The challenge would begin with 'What use were amphibious forces since amphibious landings such as D-Day were too costly in terms of casualties to be a credible option in modern times?' The response would be that a key role for modern amphibious forces was to *avoid* opposed landings such as Normandy. The Task Group would use its mobility to position where the enemy least expected amphibious landings. I would then go on to explain how the *Cougar* group – thanks to its construct with the LCG at its core – was able to plan a wide range of operations from amphibious landings to non-combatant evacuations and everything in between.

The focus then shifted to questioning the running costs of the Royal Navy's helicopter carriers. With *OCEAN* entering refit and *ILLUSTRIOUS* now the high-readiness helicopter carrier we had in any case to take a decision on which of the two offered the best long-term solution to providing the capability until the new generation of carriers entered service. The recommendation was relatively straight-forward to make. *OCEAN* was 16 years younger than *ILLUSTRIOUS*, had a 394 smaller ship's company and had proved its versatility during the Libya campaign. As a result running on *OCEAN* was the most cost-effective and sensible choice. We were challenged to explain why we needed a helicopter carrier at all – couldn't we do without until the new carriers arrived? Once again we were back to the mandated need for a scalable Maritime Task Group based around a Commando Group Littoral Manoeuvre capability. The requirement was to land a company of Marines by helicopter and for this you needed a large flat deck – another would be landed by surface means (landing craft). Walking away from this commitment so soon after it was made in the

SDSR simply was not tenable – especially after the capability had so convincingly proved itself off Libya.

The role of HMS *ALBION* and *BULWARK* (LPDs) was also tested. And here the mistake was to base their capability purely on the landing craft they carried – this capability could be provided with much cheaper and more lean-crewed ships such as the Bay-class auxiliaries. However, *ALBION*'s main role was not surface lift but command and control and these ships even today are the Navy's most capable command and control platforms – not only for amphibious and naval operations but also potentially for a joint commander. The fact that they have two additional large helicopter spots and eight landing craft simply increases their versatility. Once the explanation was given the future of these ships was not challenged again while I was DNRP.

The next question was one of protected mobility, provided by the Viking All-Terrain Vehicle. An amphibious vehicle, it was the only protected vehicle designed to fit in the UK's shipping and therefore was an important enabler for the Lead Commando Group. The issue we faced in 2011 was that the Viking fleet had since 2006 been extensively used in Afghanistan (by the Royal Marines and Army) and were now in need of extensive refit. The work was not overly expensive at some £37M but again we were questioned on whether the Lead Commando Group needed protected mobility at all. Once again, I was able to use the Libya deployment to explain how protected mobility had been a key factor in our planning to use 40 Cdo to secure the port facilities in Misrata. Crucially my argument was strongly supported by the Head of Army RP, Alistair Dickinson. As the various capability areas were being divided and apportioned to the front line commands, protected mobility rightly fell to the Army and Alistair's overwatch. He was clear that the LCG was a high-priority Defence output and as such Viking refurbishment sat high on the Army's priority list – even though it would be operated by the Royal Marines. In the face of some opposition this joined-up approach – and the careful use of an underspend by the First Sea Lord – ensured that the work went ahead.

Alistair and I were also tasked to analyse the structure of the Lead Commando Group and to identify where efficiencies in Army manpower could be achieved. The work highlighted the cost-effective nature of the RM Commando generation process. Since they were part of the Naval Service naval harmony rules applied to their terms and conditions, meaning that they could be deployed for up to 660 days in any three years compared to 498 days for the Army. Put another way, the Royal Marine Commando units would be in a 1-in-3 cycle compared to a 1-in-5 cycle for equivalent Army units. 40 Cdo's rapid turnaround from Afghanistan to deploy on *Cougar* would have breached Army rules. We did manage to recommend a dual hatting of some of the supporting artillery assets but the LCG construct survived relatively unscathed. Alistair and I established that it was a cost-effective organisation that – as Libya proved – provided considerable flexibility for contingent operations. Together we also ensured that the Apache helicopters also received some modest modifications for the marine environment – such as additional flotation gear to increase the chances of the crew getting out of the aircraft if it ditched.

The next major issue with which DNRP grappled was carrier strike. SDSR 2010 had announced that we would operate only one aircraft carrier and that would be equipped with catapult and arrestor gear, known as cats and traps.[1] The second carrier might be held at extended readiness to regenerate to ensure a continuous carrier strike capability or alternatively it might be sold. The fate of the second carrier would be decided in the next SDSR planned for 2015. On arriving back in the MOD the immediate issue was the cost of fitting catapults and arrestor gear into the ships. The plan was to fit them into the second carrier HMS *PRINCE OF WALES* meaning that the first carrier would, on entering service, be unable to operate fasts and would enter reserve on arrival of its more capable sister. However, in under two years from the SDSR decision the estimated costs of fitting cats and traps in one ship doubled from £1BN to £2BN and would delay the introduction of carrier strike from 2020 to 2023.[2] The utility and future of the unmodernised *QUEEN ELIZABETH* would be limited and continuous carrier strike capability unachievable.

The financial costs and the delays in the introduction of carrier strike resulted in the decision to revert to STOVL F35B jets announced on

10 May 2012.[3] In DNRP we had produced much of the briefing used by ministers, officials and the Navy to support the announcement. For me the opportunity this decision presented was a result of the fact that both unconverted carriers would be able to operate the same STOVL fast jets. This provided us with the option to bring both ships into service ensuring continuous carrier strike capability and periods when the second deck might also be used in the helicopter carrier role. This would be an increase in capability from that envisaged in the SDSR which stated that only one ship would be in service and the other in extended readiness (or indeed sold). My argument was based on both capability and value for money – and with the blessing of the First Sea Lord my team and I made our case to the Centre and the finance director. Put simply, the two ships had cost some £6BN to build and our research estimated that running the second carrier would cost much less than £60M per year – that included people, running and maintenance. To dispose of the second carrier – or place it in reserve – would not be a sensible return on the costs of build. We also argued that having both ships in commission would provide greater capability choice – ensuring we always had a high-readiness carrier strike platform and for the majority of the time a second carrier for training or amphibious roles. I was also able to quote Admiral Coindreau and his experience of losing *CHARLES DE GAULLE* halfway through the Libya campaign – if you are building aircraft carriers makes sure you have two because otherwise you can guarantee when you need your single carrier it will be in refit. Above all else the argument was won using detailed financial spreadsheets and in the 2015 SDSR the intention to run both carriers was announced.[4] In addition, *OCEAN* would be run on until the second aircraft carrier was in service and ready to take the amphibious role.

My three-star boss Air Marshal Stephen Hiller was also responsible for the Carrier Enabled Power Projection (CEPP) programme and overseeing the procurement/integration of all elements that would deliver the carrier strike capability. Both Richard Knighton and I provided RP advice and support to the programme as needed. Here again my Libya experience came into play. A major part of the CEPP programme was the provision of logistic support and specifically the solid stores support ship that would replace the capability provided by *FORT ROSALIE* to the Task Group. Both *FORT ROSALIE* and its sister *FORT AUSTIN* were old (commissioned in 1978/79) and importantly were incompatible with the new aircraft carriers. The requirement was for three ships (to also replace the slightly newer *FORT VICTORIA*) and in 2021 this was estimated to cost some £1.5BN. Every aspect of the programme was rightly being scrutinised and a naval officer who worked for Air Marshal Stephen had done some research that suggested that the solid store support ship was simply not required. With the equipment programme already significantly underfunded the possibility of cancelling the programme was attractive. Unfortunately, the naval officer concerned had little experience of Task Group operations and had researched how much time the Invincible-class carriers had spent in company with the store ships. Unsurprisingly the figure was very low – since the carriers had very rarely conducted high-tempo operations – but Libya, and indeed previous operations, proved that when they did the logistic support ship was essential. Thankfully the advice of the former Task Group Commander had more weight than the well-intentioned analysis and won the day – the support ships remained in the programme.

Bringing the new carriers into service would be a significant challenge to the Navy's personnel numbers. SDSR 2010 had seen the Royal Navy reduced by 3,000 people – and on a number of occasions people reductions had been made to protect platforms/maximise savings. For example, the decision to place one of the LPDs (*ALBION* or *BULWARK*) into extended readiness deleted a ship's company from the naval strength. However, every five years or so both ships would be required to be fully crewed as one ship emerged from refit and the other retained the Amphibious flagship role. Similarly, *OCEAN* was due to pay off to provide its people to assist with crewing *QUEEN ELIZABETH* – and now it was being run on until *PRINCE OF WALES* joined the Fleet. By 2012 managing people numbers was a major challenge for the Royal Navy. In DNRP we attempted to identify where we could reasonably argue for people uplifts for the service. The decision to run on *OCEAN* which had so effectively proved its versatility in 2011 had been a Defence not a naval choice. In addition, the long-term forward deployment of mine countermeasure (MCM) ships to the Gulf was still not on a permanent basis and the Navy was providing the required people from its non-existent surplus. While DNRP could not argue for the reversal of the reductions resulting from naval inputs to SDSR we were able to make the case for *OCEAN* and the MCM crews – which were agreed.

My time as Head of Naval Resources and Plans coincided with the coming delegation of the naval budget (including the future equipment programme) to the single services. Although this was not completed until I had departed it did see the Navy and the First Sea Lord (Admiral Sir Mark Stanhope) given more freedom to use in-year underspend in imaginative ways. In 2012 DNRP was able to make the case to both the First Sea Lord and the Centre for the Navy to use underspend to purchase the River-class offshore patrol vessels *SEVERN, MERSEY* and *TYNE* which were leased from Vosper for £39M. The following year the leased ice patrol ship *PROTECTOR* was similarly bought. I also saw the running on of the River class as providing another opportunity for the Navy (and Defence). The MOD had a contract with BAE Systems that guaranteed a certain number of working days per year – and in the gap between the completion of the *QUEEN ELZABETH* class and the build of the Type 26 frigates this spare capacity would be used to build five new Batch 2 offshore patrol vessels. Some argued that these would simply replace the existing River class but in DNRP we believed that they should be used to supplement the existing ships and be available to deploy worldwide. The argument gained traction in the Centre and would subsequently be what happened. I would leave DNRP in October 2013 and believe that the team and I achieved a great deal for Defence and the Royal Navy – and my Libya experience had undoubtedly helped me to make the case. Admiral Stanhope's decision to move me from COMUKTG to DNRP had been a good one.

Epilogue

After DNRP I was fortunate enough to be promoted to Rear Admiral and was destined to serve for a further seven years in joint appointments – firstly as the Director of the Development Concepts and Doctrine Centre, the MOD's strategic think tank, and then as the Deputy Commandant and finally Commandant of the Royal College of Defence Studies in London. While I missed the opportunity to serve back with the Navy proper, these appointments were intellectually stimulating and I was able to see the continued growth of real understanding between the Royal Navy, Army and Royal Air Force and the end of the inter-service rivalries and agendas that had been so apparent (and damaging) in the run-up to, and during, my time off Libya. Indeed, the way in which all the Services have embraced the arrival of the new carrier strike capability reflects this much improved relationship.

The lessons of the 2011 maritime strike continue to be reflected in the organisation and training of the current maritime battle staffs and the role and utility of the Task Group is at the centre of naval doctrine and deployments. The personal nature of command continues to be taught to every generation of commanding officer both through experience and at the Commanding Officers Designate Courses at which the lessons of 2011 are still discussed in 2022.

Finally, looking back to 1984, with hindsight, I am struck by how successfully I was prepared at each stage for whatever came next in my career and ultimately to command the Task Group off Libya. I enjoyed every minute of the journey and would commend it to any young man or woman seeking an exciting, challenging and ultimately rewarding career – irrespective of being a dustman's son or daughter or not.

Glossary

AAC	Army Air Corps
ACDS	Assistant Chief of the Defence Staff
ACT	Area capability training
AH	Attack helicopter
ASAC	Airborne Surveillance and Control
ASRM	Assault Squadron Royal Marines
ASW	Anti-submarine warfare
ATO	Air Tasking Order
AUTEC	Atlantic Underseas Test and Evaluation Centre
AWACS	Airborne Warning and Control System
CAF	Commander Amphibious Force
CAOC	Combined Air Operations Cell
CBF	Commander British Forces
CEPP	Carrier Enabled Power Projection
CINCFLEET	Commander in Chief Fleet
CJO	Chief of Joint Operations
CLF	Commander Landing Force
CO	Commanding officer
COMATG	Commander Amphibious Task Group
COMCSG	Commander Carrier Strike Group
COMOPS	Commander Operations
COMUKTG	Commander UK Task Group
CORRO	Correspondence Officer
COS	Chief of Staff
CSAR	Combat search and rescue
CTF50	Commander Task Force 50

CTG	Commander Task Group
DMC	Directorate of Media Communications
DNRP	Directorate of Naval Resources and Plans
DSF	Directorate of Special Forces
FCG	Fleet Command Group
FLF	Free Libyan Forces
FOST	Flag Officer Sea Training
HOD	Head of Department
HQDSF	Headquarters Director Special Forces
ISTAR	Intelligence, surveillance, target acquisition and reconnaissance
JFH	Joint Force Harrier
JMC	Joint Maritime Course
JTAC	Joint Terminal Air Attack Controller
LPD	Landing Platform Deck
LCG	Lead Commando Group
LCU	Landing Craft Utility
LCVP	Landing Craft Vehicle and Personnel
LSD	Landing Ship Dock
MANPAD	Man-portable air defence system
MCM	Mine countermeasure
MNSTC-I	Multi-National Security Transformation Command – Iraq
MOD	Ministry of Defence
MPA	Maritime Patrol Aircraft
MTWS	Medium Term Work Strands
NTC	National Transitional Council
OCP	Operation Commitments Plot
OPCOM	Operational Command
OPCON	Operational Control
OUT	Officers Under Training
OST	Operational sea training
PGF	Pro-Gaddafi forces

PJHQ	Permanent Joint Headquarters
PUS	Permanent Undersecretary
PWO	Principal Warfare Officer
PWO(U)	Principal Warfare Officer (Underwater)
REME	Royal Electrical and Mechanical Engineers
RFTG	Reaction Forces Task Group
RHIBs	Rigid-hull inflatable boats
RN	Royal Navy
ROE	Rules of Engagement
SBMRI	Senior British Military Representative – Iraq
SKASAC	Sea King Airborne Surveillance and Control
SO1	Staff Office Level 1
SSN	Nuclear powered attack submarine
STANAVFORLANT	NATO Standing Force Atlantic
TACOM	Tactical Command
TACON	Tactical Control
TLAM	Tomahawk Land Attack Missile
UAVs	Unmanned aerial vehicles
UKACC	UK Air Component Commander
UKMARFOR	UK Maritime Forces
UKMCC	UK Maritime Component Commander
URNU	University Royal Naval Unit
VCDS	Vice Chief of Defence
VCP	Vehicle check point
WRNS	Women's Royal Naval Service
XJ	Xray Juliet – radio callsign of the coalition maritime interdiction Commander in the Gulf
XO	Executive Officer

Royal Navy Units Involved In Cougar11/Operation *Ellamy*

Maritime Component Commander (Northwood)   Rear Admiral I. F. Corder

UK Task Group

Commander UK Task Group and Commander	Commodore J. M. L. Kingwell
Amphibious Force	
Commander Landing Force	Colonel H. White RM
HMS *ALBION* (Amphibious Assault Ship Dock)	Captain J. D. Morley
HMS *OCEAN* (Amphibious Helicopter Carrier)	Captain A. Betton
HMS *SUTHERLAND* (Type 23 Frigate)	Commander R. R. Readwin
FNS *COMMANDANT BIROT* (French Frigate)	Commander T. de Possesse
40 Commando	Lieutenant Colonel M. J. A. Jackson RM

857 Squadron (Sea King ASAC)	Lieutenant Commander G. Hayward
656 Squadron AAC (Apache)	Major W. Laidlaw AAC
RFA *MOUNTS BAY* (Landing Ship Dock)	Captain P. Farmer RFA
RFA *CARDIGAN BAY* (Landing Ship Dock)	Captain P. B. Minter RFA
RFA *FORT ROSALIE* (Stores Ship)	Captain R. G. Ferris MVO OBE RFA Captain P. Hanton RFA

Other Units

HMS *CUMBERLAND* (Type 22 Frigate)	Captain S. Dainton
HMS *LIVERPOOL* (Type 42 Destroyer)	Commander C. N. O. Williams
HMS *YORK* (Type 42 Destroyer)	Commander S. P. L. Staley
HMS *IRON DUKE* (Type 23 Frigate)	Commander N. C. R. Cooke-Priest
HMS *WESTMINSTER* (Type 23 Frigate)	Commander T. Green
HMS *TRIUMPH* (SSN)	Commander R. P. Dunn
HMS *TURBULENT* (SSN)	Commander R. T. Ramsey

HMS *BANGOR* (Mine Countermeasures)	Lieutenant Commander N. K. Marriott
HMS *BROCKLESBY* (Mine Countermeasures)	Lieutenant Commander J. Byron
RFA *ORANGELEAF* (Tanker)	Captain D. J. M. Worthington OBE RFA
RFA *WAVE KNIGHT* (Tanker)	Captain V. B. Ramsey-Smith RFA
RFA *ARGUS* (Primary Casualty Receiving Ship)	Captain D. P. Kehoe RFA

Fleet Air Arm
815, 845, 847 Naval Air Squadron

Notes

Chapter One

1   A/S/Lts Mark Darlington and Mike Robertson, Mid Mark Atkinson, Simon Pryce.
2   Leo Marriott, *Royal Navy Frigates since 1945* (Shepperton: Ian Allen Ltd, 1990).
3   HMS *EDINBURGH*, USS *MAHAN*, HNLMS *WITTE DE WITH*, BNS *WIELINGEBN*, HMCS *OTTAWA*, HNoMS *NARVIK*, FGS *EMDEN*.
4   The end of the Cold War saw this fit cancelled, and *EDINBURGH* would eventually join the rest of its class by mounting two Phalanx systems either side of the funnel.
5   Completed on 24 Aug 1956 by Whites Shipyard, Southampton.
6   S/Lt Mike Knott and S/Lt Tim Henry, later Commodore and Rear Admiral respectively.
7   Louise Midgley, 'Danish Scad Boat Fined', *Fishing News*, 24 January 1992.
8   Midshipman RNR.
9   Replaced by Chief Petty Officer (Electronic Warfare) Kevin Freestone.
10 Replaced by AB 'Buck' Taylor.
11 Lt Richard Buckland RNR, S/Lt Joe Kirk RNR and S/Lt Philip Padgham RNR.
12 Commanded by Lt Cdr Frank Wallbridge.
13 Commanded by Lt Cdr Keith Creates.
14 Commanded by Lt James Morse.
15 Since then the firefighting equipment in P2000s has been markedly improved.
16 Jon Crocker, 'Back from that trip to France', *Guernsey Evening Press*, 29 March 1993.
17 Jon Crocker, 'French abduct navy boarding Party', *Guernsey Evening Press*, 29 March 1993.
18 Vice Admiral Sir Roy Newman.
19 HMS *PURSUER* Captain's Night Order Book 29 March 1993 entry.
20 S. R. Ozanne, Letter to CINCNAVHOME, dated 13 May 1993.
21 Capt P. C. Wykeham-Martin's AH5260/004, dated 19 May 1993.
22 Lieutenant Paul Romney.
23 Early 1999.
24 UNSCR 986.

Chapter Two

1 Known as Deputy Assistant Chief of Staff (Programmes) – DACOS(Prog).
2 Vice Admiral Tim McClement.

Chapter Four

1 Brian Reyes, 'Task Force Ready for Action', *Gibraltar Chronicle*, 13 April 2011.

Chapter Five

1 Deborah Haynes and Charles Bremner, 'Britain is sending in attack helicopters to step up the battle with Gaddafi', *The Times*. 24 May 2011.
2 Tom Coghlan, 'Attack helicopters at risk from mobile missiles', *The Times*, 25 May 2011.
3 For Army units this means 'Well done!'
4 Kim Senguta 'Out of the darkness the Apaches hit...and change the game', *The Times*, 5 June 2011
5 Rob Weighill and Florence Gaub, *The Cauldron: NATO's Campaign in Libya* (London: Hurst and Company, 2018), p. 164.
6 The staff officer level (SO1, 2 or 3) denotes the rank of officer who normally delivers it. SO1 is Commander or Lieutenant Colonel, SO2 is Lieutenant Commander or Major and SO3 is Lieutenant (RN) or Captain (RM or Army).

Chapter Six

1 *The Cauldron*, p. 88.

Chapter Seven

1 *The Cauldron*, p. 194.

Chapter Eight

1 'Securing Britain in an Age of Uncertainty: The Strategic Defence and Security Review', Cm 7948 October 2010.
2 Secretary of State for Defence Philip Hammond to Parliament, Hansard, 10 May 2012.
3 Secretary of State for Defence Philip Hammond to Parliament, Hansard, 10 May 2012.
4 'National Security Strategy and Strategic Defence and Security Review 2015: A Secure and Prosperous UK', Cm 9161 November 2015.

Selected Bibliography

Crawford, Alex, *Colonel Gaddafi's Hat* (London: HarperCollins, 2012).

Laidlaw, Will, *Apache over Libya* (Barnsley: Pen and Sword, 2016).

Mitchel, Simon (ed.), *A Global Force* (Buxton: Buxton Press, 2012).

Warships International Fleet Review, *Mission Creep Libya*, and *Gaddafi Forces Lays Mines in waters off Battered Misrata Port*, HPC Publishing, June 2011.

Warships International Fleet Review. *RN Hits Gaddafi Hard*, HPC Publishing, September 2011.

Warships International Fleet Review. *RN Cougar Prowls the Oceans*, HPC Publishing, October 2011.

Weighill, Bob and Gaub, Florence, *The Cauldron: NATO's Campaign in Libya* (London: Hurst and Company, 2018).

Index

Ranks shown are those held when encountered in the book.